# THIS THING
# CALLED LIFE

# ALSO BY
# ERNEST HOLMES

# THIS THING CALLED LIFE

## Ernest Holmes

*Ernest Holmes*

*A Jeremy P. Tarcher/Putnam Book*
*published by*
*G. P. PUTNAM'S SONS*
*New York*

A Jeremy P. Tarcher/Putnam Book
Published by G. P. Putnam's Sons
*Publishers Since 1838*
200 Madison Avenue
New York, NY 10016
http://www.putnam.com/putnam

First Jeremy P. Tarcher/Putnam Edition 1997

Library of Congress Cataloging-in-Publication Data
Holmes, Ernest, 1887–1960.
This thing called life / by Ernest Holmes.
p.  cm.
Reprint: Originally published: New York: Dodd, Mead & Co., c1943.
1. New Thought.   2. Success.   3. Happiness.   4. Faith.   I. Title.
BF645.H572   1989
299'.93—dc19                    89-3654   CIP

ISBN 0-87477-867-0
Printed in the United States of America
3   5   7   9   10   8   6   4   2

*I will call this higher part of the universe by the name of God. We and God have business with each other; and in opening ourselves to His influence our deepest destiny is fulfilled.*

—William James

# Chapter I

THE WORLD is crying out for God. Lost in the canyons of disillusionment, where the trail runs out and stops against granite barriers that wall us in, we cry: "Why hast thou forsaken me?" When war devastates the land and tremblingly we stand at the mouth of hell, listening to the screaming of airplanes, the wails of the wounded, and the terror of headlines, we cry: "Why hast thou forsaken me?"

The answer to our need lies not in God's willingness, but in our will to accept, in our ability, through faith, to recognize the Divine Presence as the great reality of life. The Power of God within us is like a sleeping giant which must be awakened that it may spring into action.

What is the secret longing of your heart? If you saw an advertisement which read: *You can learn how to be well, happy and successful; you can learn how*

1

*to influence people; how to create your own destiny,* would this have a greater attraction for you than an advertisement which read: *You can learn how to help others?* or would you be even more intrigued by this advertisement: *Do you wish to become one of the molders of human destiny?*

Any one of these propositions would be attractive. We all have a desire to be well, happy and prosperous. We wish to make friends, to be respected and admired by others, and every right-minded person wishes to contribute something toward the betterment of mankind.

The one who is ill wishes to recover. An impoverished person wishes to become enriched. To the one who is unhappy, happiness stands for heaven. To the lonely, love and friendship are of the utmost importance. Upon a closer examination, however, there is one central, but perhaps unconscious and unuttered thought, running through all these desires— something big enough to include "all this and heaven too."

The greatest satisfaction in using the Law of Life is in the consciousness that such a Power is available, rather than in any use we make of It. For any particular use we make of It is a passing thing, whether it be healing oneself or others or producing any other temporary good. All of these are transitory and there is something in everyone that longs for permanency.

The artist knows that even though he has created something beautiful, it can be destroyed. His real

2

and innermost satisfaction is not in the object, but in the subject; that thing within him which penetrates the mystic splendor of Beauty itself. So it is with all our temporary creations. Empires may rise and fall. Chance and change, the vicissitudes of fortune, the comings and goings of human events, the isolated dramas of our own experiences, the temporary or more or less permanent friendships in our lives, inevitably must give way to something bigger. You are greater than the sum-total of all the experiences you have had. As Walt Whitman said, "There is more to a man than is contained between his head and his boot straps."

Your supreme satisfaction will be in the knowledge that the Law of Life exists; that you are one with It, inseparable from It. We must, then, conceive of Life as a Presence so complete that the word *Infinite*, alone, with all it implies, is adequate to express It.

There is a Universal Wholeness seeking expression through everything. We are calling it simply *Life*. The religionist calls it *God*. The philosopher calls it *Reality*. Life is infinite energy coupled with limitless creative imagination. It is the invisible essence and substance of every visible form. Its nature is goodness, truth, wisdom and beauty, as well as energy and imagination. Our highest satisfaction comes from a sense of conscious union with this invisible Life. All human endeavor is an attempt to get back to first principles, to find such an inward wholeness that all sense of fear, doubt and uncertainty vanishes.

The Science of Mind is merely one of the tools we use in giving expression to the Life Principle. Our greatest satisfaction lies not in the fact that we can use this Principle, but in the realization that such a Power exists and that we are one with It.

If we carry a light into a darkened room, the darkness is dissipated without effort on our part. So it is in the experience of one who has a deep consciousness of Life. Something invisible but all-penetrating will flow through his every look and gesture. People will feel better by sitting in his presence. Healings will take place automatically.

The Divine Spirit is not a mythical, abstract being, living somewhere above this earth. God is a Divine Presence revealing Himself to everyone who believes. Where God is recognized, there is life. Where the presence of God is realized, there is action. Where the goodness of God is acknowledged, there is peace.

We must come to understand what faith and prayer really are and how it is that God works through us. We must no longer believe that God is a God only of some one race or creed, for God is the God of all life, of everyone's life, of everything that lives. God is the intelligence, the beauty, the law and order, the animating principle in and through everything.

The unfoldment of personality is a projection of

the eternal, creative Spirit, which is the essence of all personality and the background of all individuality. Humanity proclaims divinity, while divinity unites humanity. There really is a Great Physician who can heal the diseases of the world. The power of the Spirit of God is within everyone but it must be consciously drawn upon.

The power of spiritual thought, through faith and communion, is the most dynamic power ever discovered. We did not create this power but we can use it. The Invisible passes into visibility through our faith.

Have we really tried God? Since all other methods have failed, a divine compulsion is laid upon everyone to find the power of God and make use of it. The cry: "My God, my God, why hast thou forsaken me?" rising from countless millions of anguished minds, as they hang upon the cross of human suffering, will not go unanswered if faith in the Divine Presence is gained.

It is not merely a new theory about God that we are looking for, it is the actual power of God that we must lay hold of. Our trouble is that we have not really believed that this Presence exists and operates in human affairs. We have not realized the Divine Presence as a living and dynamic reality. What we need is the direct experience of a conscious contact with the Divine.

God is Life; not some life but all Life. God is Action; not some action but all Action. God is Power;

not some power but all Power. God is Presence; not some presence but all Presence. God is pure Spirit, filling all space. This pure Spirit animates your every act. There is a real you which lives in a real God and the two are one. To know this is to understand the secret of life. To realize this is to understand your relationship with the Divine Presence. To realize that the Law of God is written in your own mind is to make available to you a power which can meet every need.

God has been called by a thousand names, but you and I, in the discussions which follow, are to think of God as Life, the presence and power in everything, which makes everything what it is. Let us use the word "Life" to symbolize everything God means to us; just the simple word "Life." Let us, then, see if we cannot discover what Life means to us and just how it operates through us. Let us discuss who and what the Self really is.

# Chapter II

I T IS said that Jesus, walking through the multitude, diffused a healing power which touched people into wholeness by its divine presence. His command stilled the wind and wave. His knowledge of spiritual law fed the thousands. His consciousness of peace calmed the troubled mind. His love was as a healing balm to the sick. Jesus possessed a transcendent power. Have you asked yourself, "Why can't I perform these same miracles? Why can't I live a life of magic?" I think you have—I have—everyone has.

Jesus consciously brought the invisible power of Life to bear upon his environment. He told his followers that what he was doing they could do if they believed they could. The whole mystery and meaning of the teaching of Jesus is bound up in the word, *believe.*

7

When we turn to the teachings of Jesus we find them direct, simple and understandable. He said: "I am come that they might have life, and that they might have it more abundantly." He was always talking about the more abundant life, the greater happiness, the deeper peace. He told us that we can rest secure in the love of God; that the power of God is always at our command. He said that God is love, God is truth, God is life, God is power. Not some life, some love, some truth, some power, but *all* life, *all* truth, *all* love, *all* power.

Jesus never claimed to be different from other men. He said: What I am you are also; what I do you can do; where I am going you may go. Did he not tell us that the kingdom of heaven is at hand? He told us that the only thing that obscured heaven is our lack of faith.

We do not know just how Jesus acquired his wonderful faith, but he must have had moments of doubt and misgiving just as we all do. He must have experienced uncertainty, just as you and I, but unlike most of us, he triumphed. He walked over the waters of doubt, the waves of confusion and the tempests of unbelief.

Jesus was a happy and radiant soul. He was triumphant. He said: I have come that ye might have joy; I have come that ye might have peace; I have come that ye might have life. Blessed are they who do hunger and thirst after the truth for they shall find it. And when someone asked him, "What is the truth?" he answered, "I am the way, the truth and the life." *What I am you may become.*

He said: If you wish to do what I am doing, follow the few simple truths I have given you. I have told you that the kingdom of God is at hand. You do not see it because you are filled with fear. Your eyes are so filled with tears that you cannot see; your ears are so dulled with confusion that you cannot hear; your minds are so weighted down with doubt that you cannot understand.

What was his remedy for all this? *Open your spiritual eyes; listen with the inner ear; open your minds.* What is it that we are to open our eyes, our ears and our minds to? What is it that we must see, hear and understand? It is something Jesus learned through silent communion with Life. The inward ear of Jesus was in tune with the divine harmony; his inward eye looked upon a spiritual universe; his human consciousness was transmuted into divine understanding as he sought for and found his union with Life.

Is it not true that we seek wholeness in externals? We should like to influence people and make friends, but have we realized that the friendship which comes through influencing people lacks that inwardness which makes friends without influencing them?

> *IF one were really unified with his true Self, there would never be any question about friendship.*

9

IF one were really unified with Substance,
    there would never be any question about
    supply.
IF one were unified with Wholeness, he
    could not be unhappy.
IF one were conscious of his union with
    Life, he would never fear death.

When the woman touched the hem of the garment of Christ, she contacted the principle of Life Itself. This contact automatically healed her. Touching Wholeness in another revealed her own wholeness.

Some day when you are confused, try this simple experiment. Sit down quietly and say:

The peace of God is at the center of my being.
I am conscious of this peace.
I enter into this peace.
I am surrounded by this peace.
This peace moves out from me in all directions.
It calms the troubled waters of my experience.
It heals everything it contacts.
There is nothing but peace.
I rejoice in this peace.
I permit this peace to enter my soul, to fill

*me with calm, to inspire me with confi-*
*dence.*
*I know that this peace goes before me and*
*makes perfect, plain and straight my way.*

No matter how many thoughts of doubt enter your mind, just mentally brush them aside. Sit in the silence of your thought until you see through the confusion. You will soon discover that just as the sun dissipates the fog, so your sense of peace will penetrate a wall of confusion. Peace already is; we merely have failed to recognize it.

*Meet every doubt that enters your mind*
*with greater faith.*
*Meet every confusion with a deeper sense of*
*calm.*
*Take the time to do this.*
*Arrange with yourself to give yourself this*
*time.*
*Start your day with peace and you will live*
*it in peace.*
*Peace is the power at the heart of God and*
*God is in you even as He is in everything.*

Life flows into everything, through everything; It passes into every human event and translates Itself through every human act. If you learn to think of Life as flowing through your every action, you will

11

soon discover that the things you give your attention to are quickened with new energy, for you are breathing the very essence of Being into them.

If you think of Life as always bringing to you everything you need, you will have formed a partnership with the Invisible which will prosper you in everything you do. If you think of the organs and functions of your physical being as activities of Life, then automatically you will be healed.

The spiritual gifts which people have so earnestly sought after, out of the anguish of their incompleteness, are not something which a reluctant deity has withheld from man. Quite the reverse. They are something which man, in his ignorance, has withheld from himself. Life is not vindictive. It is not withholding anything from you. It is not even waiting until you are good enough to receive. Life is love, beauty and wisdom, as well as energy and imagination. You will be able to use Its power in exact proportion as you embody Its essence.

The one who would heal hate must first learn to love.

> *Love is natural. Hate is unnatural. It is natural to have confidence in the universe. There is One Power and One Presence back of and in everything. This Power and Presence must become real to him. He must learn to sense It in persons and in events.*

*We tend to become like that with which we identify the self.*

The one who would live a beautiful life must commune with Beauty.

*Beauty never withheld Itself from him. It has not delivered Itself to some and withheld Itself from others. There is no such thing as a special dispensation of Beauty to any one individual or to any group, no matter what their belief may have been.*

The one who would give happiness must first become happy.

*The blind cannot lead the blind. There must be a seeing eye. Develop this inward vision. Understand who and what you are and why you cannot help being happy, and you will bring joy to everyone whom you contact.*

The one who would heal a sense of loss must first have arrived at an inner realization of wholeness.

*A part cannot heal another part; only the whole can heal its parts. You can give only what you possess.*

13

Life does not condemn; It does not punish. There is no condemnation and no judgment other than the logical reaction of our own acts. Punishment and unhappiness are logical reactions of our acts. If our acts, as they must, spring from our inward thoughts, then it follows that when we change our inward states, we shall at the same time change their sequence. That is, we shall be introducing a new law of cause and effect into our lives and the effects of our previous mistakes will disappear. This is why it has been written that there is no condemnation to them who are in Christ—to those who live in conscious union with Life, imbibing Its spirit and Its nature.

Miracles never happen. Every manifestation of faith through prayer, every wonder and sign which has followed the devotional life, has been a logical, an inevitable and an irresistible result of some cause set in motion in the Life Principle.

This in no way minimizes the effects of faith and devotion; it merely explains them. Now that we have definite knowledge of spiritual principles, we are in a position consciously to use them, and when we do, that which has been called miraculous will become an everyday occurrence.

# *Chapter III*

LIFE GOES on . . . but are we making the most of this thing called Life?

We can imagine a fish being told that he is surrounded by water but not quite realizing what this means. We can imagine such a fish swimming north, south, east and west in search of water. If we think of this fish as a person, we can even imagine him looking up the books of fish lore, studying fish psychology and philosophy, always endeavoring to discover just where the Waters of Life are and how to approach them.

Perhaps some wise old fish might say, "It has come down to us through tradition that in ancient times our ancestors knew about a wonderful ocean of life. They prophesied a day when all shall live in the Waters of Life happily forever." And can't we imagine all the other fish getting together, rolling their eyes, wiggling their tails, looking wise and mysterious and beginning to chant, "O water, water, water, we beseech you to reveal yourself to us; we beseech you to flow around and through us, even as you did in the days of our revered ancestors."

As a matter of fact, we are in the Water of Infinite Life as the fish is in the ocean. The Spirit of Life is all around us. It flows through us. It permeates everything. It is the essence of all form and flows through every condition. And yet we are still looking for It. What we look for we unwittingly look at, but fail to recognize.

Today, this minute, your mind is an outlet through which this invisible but intelligent Energy is operating. It is operating creatively through you at this very moment, and whether you know it or not, or believe it or not, today it is creating and recreating every cell of your body. It is molding and remolding every situation and condition in your environment.

The Life by which you are surrounded is the essence of all life, the substance of every form, the intelligence back of every act. It is the life in the animal, in the tree, in the mineral. It is the source of intelligence in man.

There are some truths about the nature of this Life which we must realize before we can consciously use It. First of all, Life is pure intelligence. You and I do not conceive of such an Infinite Intelligence in Its entirety, but we do conceive of It in some degree

16

because we are in and of It and some part of It is in us. Otherwise we would not and could not exist.

Life creates by making things out of Itself. Let us think of Life as pure Spirit, creating through the agency of Its word. That is, by thought or idea. The thought or idea of Life automatically becomes law; the Law of Life is a law of mind in action.

Let us start with the simple proposition that Life, which is Spirit or Intelligence, is the sole and only creative agency in the universe. This Life Principle always existed and will always continue to exist. You are part of Its self-expression, therefore the whole desire of Life is to give you more life. And since It is all life, It has all life to give you. It loves you because, in creating you, It has given some part of Itself to you. You are dear to Life, beloved by It. In creating you It has poured Itself into you. You could not ask for greater love than this and more love could not be given.

The intelligence of Life is our intelligence. It is the very presence of inspiration, guidance, direction. It is waiting for us to use It, to make Itself manifest in our lives. This does not mean that It seeks to control us. It merely waits for us to use It.

We have all been trying to find out just what our relationship to Life is, because we know by pure intuition that if we could establish a right relationship with the Invisible, we should find peace, health, harmony, prosperity and happiness. We should be able to live in the kingdom of heaven while on earth.

17

Our difficulty is that we have been trying to unite that which was never divided. We have been looking for Life outside the self. We are like the fish trying to find the Waters of Life in which it already is immersed. When Jesus said, "The kingdom of God is at hand," and when he explained that the kingdom of heaven is within, this is what he was talking about. Jesus announced the presence of God in man as well as around him.

One of the world's greatest biologists has stated that mind is the only creative agency science has ever discovered. A world-famed physicist and Nobel Prize winner has stated that science has made no discovery which contradicts the belief in an Infinite Spirit to which we have the direct relationship of being Its offspring. Jesus proclaimed the kingdom of heaven within us, God within us, the Word of God and the Power of God within us. He carefully pointed out that there is more of God than is contained in humanity. Did he not say, "It is the Father in me," while, at the same time, saying, "The Father is greater than I"?

This divine union which Jesus proclaimed, we must rediscover and make use of, for we know that God can do anything. Life has no restrictions, no limitations; It doesn't want for anything; It is perfect and It is within us. Therefore, Jesus said when you learn to be perfect in your thought and action, then you will discover that you are like God. This is what he meant when he said, "Be ye therefore perfect even as your Father which art in heaven is perfect."

One of our leading psychologists tells us that when he gets back of the individual and collective unconscious (which means the sum-total of our individual subjective reactions, plus our subjective reactions to the race mind) he discovers an entity, a person, an ego, that has never become disintegrated. Is this different from the admonition of Jesus, to be perfect even as the indwelling Spirit is perfect?

There is a wellspring of life and perfection at the center of our being upon which we may draw.

Every longing and yearning you have ever had, every secret desire of your soul, every constructive ambition you have ever had, is a whispering of this Life assuring you that you are one with It. You are a concrete manifestation, a personification of It. You are a center where Life, passing through you, becomes a definite, distinct, unique, individualization of Itself. There is no one else like you in all the universe; there never will be.

If you will take time daily to sense the presence of Life within you, to believe in It, to accept It, it will not be long before the life which you have known will gradually disappear and something new will be born —a bigger, better and more perfect you. You will pass from death into life; from lack and want into greater freedom; from fear into faith. From a sense of being alone, you will pass into a realization of oneness with everything, and you will rejoice in this oneness.

You will soon discover that when you recognize this Life in others, It will respond to you through them. It will be like calling someone by his name. It will respond and you will know that It is responding because you will feel Its response. All sense of aloneness will disappear.

Every man is some part of God, whether or not he knows or believes it, but we hypnotize ourselves into thinking that we are incomplete and imperfect. We identify ourselves with the fantastic pictures of our morbid dreams, but the ropes that bind us are ropes of sand.

Let us cease to wonder what made the machinery get out of order and spend our time in the positive realization that there is a divine mechanic at the center of our being who can repair it. Having thoroughly cleansed our mental house, we must get a new tenant, one who knows how to live in it, one who knows that he is living in the House of God—he is in heaven now, he is a guest of the Infinite.

Let us keep it as simple as this. There is but One Life and we are using It. If you follow this method, the time will come when your problem of evil will be solved. You will see through it definitely and easily, simply and directly, and you will know that all forms of evil—that is, lack, unhappiness, fear, sickness, etc. —are not things in themselves, they are merely effects of our misuse of the One Life.

There may be some who think that before they can accept this position they must become profound philosophers, spiritual sages or men of such deep scientific understanding that they stand apart from the rest of the world. This is not true. What the wisest have known is only a little more than you and I know. They cannot answer your questions for you; you will have to answer them yourself. Even the best man who ever lived could not live for you; you will have to live for yourself. You do not have to borrow power from anyone.

You are compelled to live your own life, to think your own thoughts, to experience your own being. Start with this simple proposition:

*Life is.*
*It is natural goodness and kindness.*
*It is peace, joy and wholeness.*
*I live in this Life.*
*This Life flows through me.*
*This Life is in everyone and in everything.*
*Therefore, I am one with all that is—all people, all things, all events.*

You are using the Law of Life every time you think. No matter how long you may have been using It wrongly in your ignorance, the very day, that hour, yes the very moment, you begin to use this Power rightly, the effects of having used It wrongly will pass from your experience. Does it make any difference how long a room has been dark when you introduce a light; how long the earth has been parched when refreshing rains come to bring new life, a new seed time and a new harvest to the fields?

This is where faith plays its greatest role. Without faith it is impossible for one to do his best or get the most out of life. This does not mean faith in the personality only, but faith in the ocean of Life Itself. No one has ever found a substitute for this faith. Faith in the self as an isolated being automatically cuts us off from the main stream of Life. I have never yet known a man whose faith in himself, just as an individual, or as a person, was great enough to meet the issues of life. I have met many who have tried this, but as yet I have never seen that it proved successful. There is something about our very nature that demands a constant communion with the Invisible.

Because Life is in you, then the Truth is in you, and the Spirit is in you, and Power is in you. If you will wait on this Power, this Truth and this Light, they will guide you. One of the greatest things you can do is to learn to wait on the God Power within you. Having felt the presence of this Divine Reality we are next privileged to use the Law of Its being. Begin right now by saying:

> *I know that the Spirit goes before me and*
> *makes perfect, plain, direct and immedi-*
> *ate my way.*
> *I rest in calm peace and in absolute cer-*

*tainty that all the good there is, is de-*
*voted to my well-being.*

*I know this is the truth about everyone.*

*I view myself as a part of the divine union of*
*all things. Therefore I know that I am one*
*with every person, every event, every sit-*
*uation, that arises in my experience.*

*I know that I bring forth from all persons*
*and events which I contact, the best that*
*is in them.*

*I know that I give back the best that is in*
*me.*

Since you are fundamentally a mental being, you can think yourself into being unhappy and depressed, or you can think yourself into being glad. Did it ever occur to you that you can also think yourself into being well? Into being prosperous? That you can think yourself into success? Well, you can if you believe in the Law of Life and use It rightly. But you must learn to use It affirmatively. You must learn to identify yourself with your desires.

You must become the master of your own thinking. This is the only way you will realize freedom and joy. Therefore, you will have to turn your thoughts away from lack, want and limitation, and let them dwell on good. *Make* yourself do this. Learn to think about what you wish to become.

You are a thinking center in Life, and the chief characteristic of the Law of Life is that It responds to thought. Your slightest thought sets up a vibration in It, sets Its creative intelligence in motion, and causes It to create circumstances for you which will correspond to your thought.

If most of your reactions are unhappy or morbid; if you have a great deal of illness, limitation and unhappiness in your life; if you are surrounded by unfriendly circumstances and situations, whether of people or of things, then no doubt a great part of your subconscious reactions have been of a negative character. But do not let this discourage you. That is merely the way you have been using the Law of Life.

You have free will. You are an individual. You can start today and build a new law of attraction within yourself. You can so recognize the presence of Life in everything you do, say and think, that you can create a new environment, new circumstances, here, now, and quickly. No one else can do this for you as well as you can do it for yourself. Then decide to think happiness and peace. Keep this secret within yourself—it is sacred to yourself—it is the true *Holy of Holies* within you. You have the power.

You do not have to beseech Life to be good or to bring good into your life. Life is like the sun. It shines on everything. Get out of the shadows! Crawl out of your basement! Open the windows of your mind! Open the doors of your soul! Lift up your thought and let Life be to you whatever you wish It to be! Learn to resurrect yourself! Let us see just how this is done.

# Chapter IV

THE ONE who learns how to control his thinking, learns how to control his destiny. We are bound by our own thought world. Nothing can save us but ourselves. The individual who will learn how consciously to change his thinking processes can remold his destiny.

Negative forces operating in our lives will die a natural death if we practice the habit of being disinterested in them. All outward forms of behavior are automatic results of inner mental picturings, be these pictures conscious or unconscious.

We are continuously being drawn into situations or circumstances, sometimes against our objective will, but seldom against our unconscious willing. Most of our mental imagery is unconscious. It comes either from previous experiences or the experiences of the race. There is much in the subconscious of which the intellect is not aware, but one thing is certain, our subjective or unconscious thought patterns can be changed. We have created them and we can change them.

The mind is a magnet and we attract that with which we identify the self. In order to get the most out of life we must learn consciously to change many of our habitual thought patterns. This is not easy, for our old thought patterns cling to us with great tenacity, but, being thought patterns, they can be reversed. If you are filled with fear, refill yourself with faith, for faith always overcomes fear.

You will soon learn, if you make the experiment, that one kind of thought can neutralize another, can rub it out. For instance, if something within you says, "I am unhappy this morning," you can deny this statement and affirm its opposite, and you will soon find that a new thought reaction takes its place. You will discover that the denial of the wrong condition causes it to disappear, while the affirmation of the right condition creates that condition.

What if we are unhappy and afraid? These dim shadows of a false identity are dissipated when the flow of Life, of spiritual realization, finds entrance to the mind. Our fears, morbidities and phantoms flee as the mist before the sun.

We cannot live without God. Every attempt to do this has failed. No fear can remain where faith holds sway. Faith reunites us with the original, creative Spirit, the Divine Mind, which already exists at the center of our being. This kingdom of heaven, which is the kingdom of wholeness, is within.

You must have a faith in something greater than your previous experiences. You must bind yourself back in faith to the God Principle within you. If we come daily to the supreme Source of all life; if we let the dead bury their dead; if we forget the impositions placed upon us by our own imaginations, or the dictatorial attempts of life to replace the joy which belongs to everyone, we shall soon plunge into the ocean of our being where wholeness and peace abide forever.

Don't be afraid of being spiritual. Since earliest history men have felt the presence of Life, believed in It and communicated with It, and they have received direct answers from It. Our difficulty lies not so much in contradicting this truth, as in cultivating an inner awareness, a deep spiritual realization that we are one with all the Presence and all the Power that there is.

Learn to clear your thought of everything that obstructs your belief in the goodness and the giving-ness of Life. Realize that the kingdom of heaven is at hand; that God wishes you to have everything worth while in life. The longings and desires for betterment, which we all experience, are but prophecies of their own fulfillment.

The Life within us awaits our acceptance of It.

The key-note of thought in every corner of our mind and in every fibre of our being should be that Life works in and through us.

> *Learn to see through confusion into peace;*
> *to see through sickness into health;*
> *to see through poverty into success*
> *and abundance;*
> *to believe in the all-sustaining Good.*
> *Learn to trust in God and be at peace.*

We shall not be less practical because we are more spiritual. We should deepen our faith and increase our vision. Let us build around us a wall of spiritual realization and therein dwell.

There are certain fundamental erroneous conclusions which we must get rid of. We must cast out of consciousness every form of fear, every belief in devil, hell, future punishment or divine vindictiveness. Our refusal to admit the reality of such beliefs is a denial of them.

There is no separation from the One Self. Our true self is Life. Since Life is the real *you*, then the real *you* is already perfect. Life knows no obstruction, so when an apparent obstruction appears, deny that it has any reality. When you deny anything that appears to be wrong, you are merely affirming the presence of the real you. Your denials and affirmations tend to build up a new and a better recognition of this real you.

A mental denial acts as an eraser rubbing out false impressions, while constructive affirmation identifies the self with God and permits Life to flow through us, fresh from the source of Its infinite wisdom and love.

Let us examine what a mental denial really does:

*It causes us to think straight.*
*It erases false opinions.*
*It removes obstructions of thought.*
*It washes the windows of the soul and lets in*
*the light.*
*Life is Light, and in that Light there is no*
*darkness.*

When we use statements similar to these we are giving our subconscious self a spiritual bath. We are bathing in the sunlight of peace, poise and power. We are cleansing the slate of our mind that new impressions may be made upon it. This does not mean that we obliterate the book of memory, for this would be both unnecessary and impossible. What we are erasing is the morbid belief that we are separated from Life. What we are denying is a mistaken belief.

*Life is not pleased by our being unhappy.*
*God is not honored by our being sad.*
*Spirit is not stimulated by our entreaty.*
*The Divine is not conditioned by our sense*
*of limitation.*

*God is, was, and remains perfect.*
*God is ready, able and willing to do any-*
  *thing for us.*
*But—the Spirit cannot give us what we re-*
  *fuse to accept.*

Because Life has equipped us with creative ability, because we are individuals, our negative thoughts can bring temporary discomfort. Otherwise we would not be free. If we can only get this firmly in mind, that Life is always for us, It is never against us; that there is no fundamental power of evil, the only and original Power is good, then we shall gain freedom.

All evil is either a misuse of this Power or a misunderstanding of It. Everything that is wrong in our experience, whether we call it pain, sickness, poverty or unhappiness, is a denial of the allness of God. Life has no adversaries, therefore, when we deny evil we are not fighting reality. The denial is like straightening out a mathematical problem. We are not fighting the wrong conclusion, we are merely explaining why it is not true. We are rearranging our thought in a way that proves to us that Life never limits us.

It is not the intellect alone with which we deal. There is a deep feeling center within us. This deep feeling center must be aroused. No matter what the intellect affirms, unless this deep feeling center accepts its statements, we shall not get very far. On the other hand, we may be certain of this: daily and consciously explaining to one's self what he believes about Life will gradually awaken this inner feeling to an acceptance of what the intellect affirms.

Life is the One Perfect Unity from which everything proceeds, including yourself and all your experiences. All action proceeds from It; all knowledge is in It. It is in us. We are in It.

The key to our whole understanding of Life lies in the realization that Life Itself is pure Spirit, is an ocean of unmanifest Being whose nature it is to take form. When the Bible states that the Word of God moves upon the face of the deep and produces creation, it means that the Divine Spirit speaks Itself into existence by the power of Its word. When the Bible states that man is made in the image and likeness of God it is telling us that each one of us, as an individual, reproduces the creative imagination and energy of the Divine Mind.

When Jesus said that the kingdom of heaven is within, he was telling us that our approach to Life is through an interior awareness. When he told us that God within us is already perfect, he was telling us what has since been rediscovered in the Science of Mind, that there is a Principle of Perfection at the center of every man's life.

We are either going to accept these things as theories about some nebulous and theoretical spiritual existence, or else we are going to accept them as Jesus meant them to be accepted, as real and actual facts in the life we live here and now. The genius of the new Science of Spirit, which is destined to save the world, is its direct approach to God and its conscious use of God Power in every activity of living.

Jesus used this Power directly and spoke It into being consciously, and because he had perfect faith in It, he performed miracles. He healed the sick, raised the dead, stilled the wind and waves and brought the boat immediately to the shore. You and I can do the same thing if we believe that we can. Jesus said that all things are possible to those who believe.

Jesus viewed the world, not as a solid fact, but as a liquid form. He viewed life not as a physical fact, but as a set of spiritual laws. He thought of Life as an invisible, interior presence, ever responding to us, but, of a necessity, responding to us through our belief. Jesus believed that he was the son of God; he believed in the power of his word, and his belief was justified by his works. No one brought up in the Christian philosophy doubts the power which Jesus exercised nor the authority with which he used it.

If you analyze your thought you will make this remarkable discovery: you already believe in Life; you already have faith in It; but you do not, perhaps, believe that you have access to the power Jesus used, or that you speak with the same authority. The thing that hinders this belief and this authority is, of necessity, a thing of thought.

The doubt that keeps us from a full use of the power of Life is either an intellectual inability to think spiritually or a subjective conditioning which blocks the passage of thought. In any event it can be reduced to mental states. Whatever can be reduced to a mental state can be changed by an opposite mental state.

The pathway of freedom, the key to success, and the consciousness which can break down the doors of our self-imposed prison, all lie in the realization that the Word of Life flows through us into manifestation. Because we are conditioned by false thinking, by every form of belief in limitation and fear, we subjectively react in a restricted manner. The very creative power which we possess is used destructively. Now we must resolve to watch our thought processes, to boldly rearrange them after a more divine pattern. This calls for self-re-education but it is not as difficult as it seems.

We not only have the ability to do this but we have the tools with which to do it. The power is faith, the tools are thoughts and ideas. Let us then learn how to use them.

# *Chapter V*

Y OU ARE now about to enter into the greatest experience of your life—a conscious use of the God Power that is within you.

*You are going to have great joy in doing this.*
*You are going to receive untold good.*
*You are going to live affirmatively.*

We have discussed the nature and use of mental denial. Now let us talk about affirmation. In the Science of Mind a denial is a conscious repudiation of that which is not true about the Life Principle, while an affirmation is a conscious recognition of that which is true.

We must learn to live by inspiration. That means that we should let the spiritual depths of our being flow through our conversation and into our acts. Living by inspiration does not mean living chaotically. Our whole purpose is to make the intellect an instrument for the Spirit. This is exactly what an artist does. We must all become artists in living. To live by inspiration means to sense the divine touch in everything; to enter into the spirit of things; to enter into the joy of living.

In our ignorance we try to find our center outside the self. This can never be. The ancients said that God's center is everywhere and His circumference no-where. We are like the upward thrust of a wave. We look about seeing other waves, apparently dissociated from us, but underneath is the One Ocean pushing all waves upward. There is One Mover in every movement, one undulating passion for self-expression.

The moment one realizes he can use the creative power of his thought to free himself from bondage, that moment he starts on a new adventure. He is giving birth to a new possibility. In time he discovers that he has built his prison walls himself; that the cell in which he has been incarcerated was self-created. By identifying himself with the spiritual universe, these walls crumble and he sees himself as a free soul. Bondage and freedom are ours to do with as we will.

Only as we give the best we have to every passing experience can we hope to enter into the joy of living. Can anyone enjoy a game unless he enter into the spirit of that game? Every act of life should be a magical rite filled with wonder; every coming event should arouse pleasurable anticipation. Whatever we do, the whole of us should be engaged in doing it. There are no half measures to living. Life itself has no adversary; It has no limitation. Consequently It speaks a straight affirmative language only.

It would be impossible to explain the external world without supposing an internal one. The mind or soul stuff which takes form through the impulsion of spiritual energy, can be conceived of only in the terms of consciousness.

We might say that in the beginning there was Mind and that this Mind is synonymous with God, with design and cosmic order. In such degree as we consciously or unconsciously unify with this Cosmic Mind, we prosper. In such degree as we oppose It, we are automatically stopped.

Just as water purifies itself as it flows, so the impure stream of our mental life becomes purified by applied constructive thinking. It may well be that a lack of circulation in the physical body is a result of mental stagnation, while mental stagnation is the result of a lack of spiritual perception.

The fate we believe in we bring to pass. This is true both individually and collectively. Just as an individual can change his destiny by revamping his thought processes, so when a sufficient number of a group change their trends of thought, the conduct of that group will also become changed. If the majority of persons living sincerely believed that the whole world could become prosperous and happy, the world would soon find a way to become both happy and prosperous.

Can you imagine a power so great that it is both an infinite presence and a limitless law? If you can you are drawing close to a better idea of the way Life works. Most of the bibles of the world have said that all things are formed by Its word. This word has been called the Secret Word, the Lost Word. It is said that some of the ancients had a holy scroll upon which was inscribed the sacred and the secret name of Life. This scroll was supposed to have been put in an ark, in a chest, and laid away in a place which was called the Holy of Holies, the innermost room of the temple.

What do you suppose was inscribed upon this sacred scroll? Just this: the words "I Am." Here is a concept of the pure, simple and direct affirmation of Life making everything out of Itself. This is why most of the scriptures have stated that all things are made by the Word of God.

Did you ever stop to think that everything that is visible is projected into form by some invisible power? Now, what do you suppose could take One Substance, One Law, One Presence and One Power and make an infinite variation of things? It would be impossible to conceive of anything doing this other than Life speaking Itself into existence through many ideas.

This is what is meant by the words "I Am." Life

says "I am this" and "I am that," and immediately *this* and *that* appear, begin to take form according to law. Life always works in accord with law. It is intelligence plus law. It is law plus conscious volition. It is law plus will and choice.

Life works by direct affirmation. There is no other way for It to work. This is why we are told to be still and know that all things are possible to God. We are told to affirm, positively to assert, to declare this truth, in the face of all apparent opposition; to claim abundance in the midst of poverty; to affirm health in the midst of sickness; to decree joy in the midst of sorrow; and to announce the kingdom of God here and now.

Why are we told to do this? Because this is the way Life works. It knows nothing about discord or fear; It forever sings the song of Its own being. This song bursts forth from the joy of Its own inner wholeness. We, too, could become part of this celestial choir if we knew how rightly to affirm Life.

What is it we are going to affirm? We are going to affirm that Life is good. We are going to do this even though everything we see and touch seems to contradict the Allness of Life. We are going to be still and know that our being is derived from pure Spirit; that God Himself is our host and that we are not strangers on the shores of time, but divine beings, guests of the kingdom of Good.

It is normal to believe in God. It is natural to believe that good has more power than evil; that love can heal hate. What if we have been disappointed and chagrined? What if we have suffered many disillusionments, many emotional embarrassments? Let us not forget that darkness has no power over light. Just as the warm rays of the sun will melt the largest iceberg, so a persistent inner perception of the abiding Over-Presence will heal our fears, whether they be conscious or subjective; will straighten out our repressions, be they ever so deeply buried in the unconscious.

To live in conscious communion with Life, even for a short time, will convert our fears into faith, our doubts into certainty, our hurt and sense of failure into something triumphant. There is a sublime and a divine hope for everyone who is willing to surrender himself to the great Good; to the warm embrace of the "Over-Soul" in whose lap, Emerson tells us, we lie as in the lap of an Infinite Intelligence. Every man has a subliminal depth to his being. We can plant our feet firmly on this faith and realize that we are divine beings now. The choice is ours.

There is but One Creative Principle. It is always responding to us. There is but One Power and we are using It either negatively or affirmatively. The great affirmation is the affirmation of the goodness and the givingness of this Power.

Just as you can deny an experience out of existence, so you can affirm an experience into existence. By affirmation, we mean to assert something, to decree something, to announce something. You will

39

soon discover that you can look a certain negative condition squarely in the face and by definitely denying it and definitely affirming its opposite, produce an opposite result. How can this be unless your thought is creative? Well, your thought *is* creative. This is the secret of life. This is the principle you are going to demonstrate.

Your thoughts are tools that you use in affirming the creative Power into your experience. You are going to make the affirmation, but the Law of Life is going to produce the result. Never forget this. It is not by holding thoughts that you accomplish good results; it is by thinking right thoughts and then loosing them into the Law of this Power. The Law of Life acts upon them in some way which you know not of. Moreover, you do not have to know. Whatever you affirm, It will do for you, provided your affirmation is in accord with Truth.

It may seem strange at first to think that we can affirm something into existence where nothing seemed to be. But is not this true when we draw a picture, mold a form, or plant a seed? Anyone wishing to demonstrate the availability of the Law of Life must certainly accept the dynamic reality of affirmation. *Affirmation is the greatest and fundamentally the only creative agency in the universe.* Everything that is, whether we realize it or not, is some affirmation of Life. You are the affirmation of this Life as individuality, as personality. This is why your thought is creative.

An affirmation is not an affirmation unless it is inwardly believed in. Hence, your intellect, your will and your feeling must agree with your affirmations if they are to have real power. Otherwise, they will be empty words. So, when you say, "The presence of Life is goodness," you are saying, "God is good. The Spirit is good. Life is good to me. Everywhere I go I meet goodness and consideration and loving-kindness."

We should not only hitch the wagon of our hope to a star, we should likewise identify our mind with the Infinite. God cannot fail and we shall cease failing when we identify ourselves with this supreme Source. Unless we do this we are making negative use of the greatest creative force we have, which is feeling and imagination.

It is well known to the Science of Mind that we tend to become like that with which we identify ourselves. If a man identifies himself with failure he becomes attracted to negative circumstances, people, etc. If he identifies himself with success he tends to become attracted to that which is successful, prosperous and happy.

Always we are brought back to this fundamental truth, that life is a mirror and that external happenings are objective correspondences of inner contemplations. *Our external world is not external at all; it is all internal but contained within a Cosmic Mind to which each one of us has a kinship,* a kinship so intimate that each may consider It personal to himself.

41

A person would not be normal unless he wished to express joy and happiness, unless he wished fulfillment. The whole problem is to find self-expression through constructive channels of thought and action.

The very last word in the Science of Mind and in psychology is a complete affirmation of the presence of Life in you as a person—uncaught, unbound, limitless and free. When psychologists study the operation of the human mind they are merely studying the action of this principle in the human mind.

We are called upon consciously to unite our thought with the Law of this Power—to do so for definite purposes; to bring health, happiness and prosperity into our lives or into the lives of others. We wish to make some sick person well. Perhaps we wish to bring happiness into a life which is destitute of joy. Possibly we wish to bring prosperity into the life of a friend who has been living in poverty. We can do all this if we believe that we can. Our belief that we can is our great affirmation about the Power. We can because *It* can.

The Law of Life is a law of mind, of Spirit, or thought. You may call it a law of cause and effect. You may call it a law of polarity. It has been called by all these terms and many more. The Law of Life says that whatever you mentally affirm, and, at the same time, become inwardly aware of, Life will create for you.

You can use this Law for yourself or others by merely directing it. Your intention, direction and recognition of this Power operating through a certain individual or situation, causes It to manifest there rather than somewhere else. If this were not true, it would be impossible to help anyone with this Power, and since this has been done in countless thousands of cases, we know that the principle involved is true.

In using the Law of Life you do not merely make a lot of abstract statements, such as saying, "God is good," "God is all there is," "God is love." Such statements affirm your belief in the goodness and the allness of Life. They are necessary as a foundation for your definite work. But when you wish to help someone through the use of this Law you add to your statements that God is all Life, the thought that because God is all Life it necessarily follows that the Life of God is now flowing through the person you wish to help.

Power must be power to something; God must be God to something; consciousness must be conscious of something. The electrician does not merely say, "There is enough electric energy to light this building"; rather it is because he knows that there is enough electric energy to light the building that he wires the building and connects it with the power station. When you are seeking to help someone else you are not the power station; you are not the wires; you are not the energy, but you are using it for definite purposes.

The following is an illustration of the use of this Power.

Being a student of the way the Life Principle works, she couldn't understand why she had been unable to demonstrate supply through the channel of her chosen profession. She was always saying, "God is all there is. God is the only Mind there is. God is the only Presence there is." She labored under the misapprehension that abstract statements can produce definite results. No greater mistake could be made in dealing with the Law of Life. We must *always connect* the Law with what we are doing. This she had never done. That was why she had failed to demonstrate.

Building upon the conviction she already possessed, I taught her to think in the following manner: "I have a service to render. My business is to teach the piano. Whoever needs my service, whomever I can peculiarly and personally benefit, those whom I can particularly aid in this art, are irresistibly drawn to me now, today, this moment."

There is no state of futurity in the Law of Life, therefore all statements should be an affirmation of the present. I taught her to live in the expectancy that wherever she went she would meet people who would desire her assistance, who would be glad to have it, and who would be able justly to compensate for her services. This was an entirely new lineup and one she had never thought of or used before. I assured her that her belief in the Infinite was right, her statements about God were correct, but that she had not, in a certain sense, joined heaven and earth into

44

one harmonious unity. I told her to expect to meet people wherever she went who would require her services.

A few months after having kept these ideas in mind, she told me that if she sat down beside a stranger invariably he began to talk to her and it always followed that he would ask what she did, which gave her the opportunity to talk about her profession. On quite a number of occasions she secured pupils in this way. She found pupils at parties, in the theatre, on the street. All at once her friends seemed to remember what her profession was and began to send pupils to her.

Of course I explained that there is no magic in any formula, but that, nevertheless, certain mental methods of procedure persisted in and believed must produce definite results.

The Law of Life operates through your affirmation. Nothing can hinder Its working but yourself. There is no more of It on the desert than there is on the busiest street corner, and It will not respond any more quickly because we go up into the temple. It is everywhere, therefore It is where you are, and, most of all, It responds where you recognize It.

Would it be too much to say that your recognition of It makes possible Its response through you? This, indeed, is the secret of faith. Faith is the supreme affirmation. It is the unconditioned affirmative. It is the affirmation which makes all things possible to the one who believes in the Power of God.

Know that nothing can hinder you but yourself. If you believe that you can, you can. If you believe that the Law of Good will work, It will work. You are not changing the nature of Its power; you are merely altering your position in It. You cannot fail if you start with the proposition that Life is all there is. It is all the presence, law and order there is. It is the substance of every form and the law back of every fact. As the invisible, It is the cause. As the visible, It is the effect.

Demonstration means bringing some good into your life or into the experience of someone else. If you are treating someone, you are seeking to demonstrate that evil, limitation, fear and want cannot remain in his experience. Mental treatment is a mental act, an act of thought or consciousness on the part of someone whom we call a practitioner. You are a practitioner if you are using this principle consciously.

In the Science of Mind, which is a conscious use of the creative energy of the Law of Life, mental treatment is the art, the act, and the science of using this Law for the purpose of producing a definite, objective, manifest result.

Mental treatment is a thing of conscious thought, whether this thought is for yourself or directed for someone else. In your mind you are making certain affirmations and denials, which we have already explained, and seeking to reach a place of realization, acceptance, belief and faith, which, without any further contradiction in your own thought, can positively affirm the presence of Life acting as freedom, unrestricted abundance, perfect health, etc.

Treating someone present with us in the same room is called a present treatment. Treating someone at a physical distance is called an absent treatment. Since there is no absence of the divine creative Spirit, absent and present treatments are identical.

In giving this treatment you are not talking to the one you wish to help. You are making statements about him. He is already identified in Life through his name. Therefore, when you speak the name of the person you wish to help, this identifies your treatment with that person and not with someone else. After having spoken his name, your statements are made about him and not to him. For instance, you would say, "He is thus and so," rather than, "You are thus and so." You are making your declarations about him.

If you are using the Law of Life to establish health in someone's experience, you would seek to realize this Power as the presence of health. Perhaps the one you are seeking to aid may have heart trouble. If there is but One Life, then there is but One Heart. Of course, everyone has an individualized heart, but Heart itself is a divine idea of Life. You affirm the presence of this divine idea, the perfect pulsation, the perfect rhythm of Life.

Know that:

47

*There is no trouble in the one perfect Life.*
*There is no discord or fear.*
*There is no inaction, over-action or wrong*
  *action.*
*The pulsation of this Life is rhythmic.*
*The heart of reality is not troubled.*

There is one heart common to all men. This is the Heart of Reality, the Heart of God, the Heart of the Universe. It never was worn out. It never was tired. Then, mentioning the name of the person you wish to help, declare that this is the truth about him. You have entered into the great affirmation of Life. It is now the business of the Power to execute this decree and you may have implicit confidence that It will do so.

# Chapter VI

SHE WAS trying to break into the motion picture profession, but knew of no way to crash the gates, and had become discouraged. She came to me all in a heap. Discouragement and despair had reduced her to a state of hopelessness. But she did have faith, a good old-fashioned, orthodox faith.

We have little to add to such conviction as hers, but it needs direction. After all, simple, trusting faith is the greatest thing in life. Let each seek Reality in his own way and if he is sincere, surely that Presence, to which the very hairs of our heads are numbered, will honor his approach.

Knowing that each is justified in his own belief, I said to her, "Let us unite on this affirmation: 'I will set him up on high because he hath known my name.'" This thought had a definite meaning to both of us; we could each agree with it. For each of us it meant that we are surrounded by an Infinite Presence which responds to our confidence in It.

I could have gone into an elaborate explanation, telling her that the very nature of this Law of Life compelled It to respond by exact correspondence. I could have talked to her about the law of cause and effect, or the principle of reflection or polarity. But this would have had no meaning to her at that time, although it did come to have a meaning later. I merely said, "Let us take this thought: 'I will set him up on high, because he hath known my name.'" I told her that we would try to realize that setting her up on high meant that newspapers and billboards throughout the country would some day carry her name in a prominent position.

It is not the exact words used, but their meaning, which gives power to spiritual mind treatments. In a most simple and childlike way, with a complete mental abandonment of trust and faith, she repeated these words after me: "I will set him up on high, because he hath known my name."

I asked her to practice the habit of mentally seeing herself as she would like to be; definitely to stop identifying herself with failure, to know that every doorway of opportunity was open to her, to believe that every talent and ability which she possessed would be gladly recognized, welcomed, used and properly compensated for.

It worked like a charm. There was nothing in her which denied what she was affirming. Her whole being accepted it with a joyous expectancy. This is exactly the attitude of thought we should have. We must believe, as Jesus said, that when we make known our requests we already receive the answer. I have never known anyone who, in a more simple, beautiful and direct way, believed. In fact, I marveled at her faith and asked her, "Are you quite sure that you know there is a Power which will go before you and prepare the way?"

"Oh, yes," she replied, "I have always believed in God."

"Well," I said, "just keep right on. Use all the faith you have, intensify it with all the imagination and feeling you have, but never let go of your conviction. Stay with it—'I will set him up on high, because he hath known my name.' And every time you use this statement, see yourself as you would like to be."

Gradually the doors opened. The opportunity presented itself and she made good. I have no doubt that most of you have seen her perform many times.

There is a definite relationship between a successful life and one's inward thought patterns. It is impossible for one to be successful unless he mentally identifies himself with his desire. Consciously or unconsciously he must have a mental pattern of what he wishes to become.

When one who has lived in impoverishment changes his consciousness from lack to abundance, he finds a corresponding change taking place in his affairs. To identify the self with the highest success

51

and happiness, and the most permanent, we should start as the great teacher suggested, by first identifying the self with the kingdom of God, the potential possibility of all things. This statement of Jesus is really a veiled statement of the law of cause and effect. When we enter into conscious unity with the invisible Cause, the reaction will be a more abundant life. It could not be otherwise.

If one were to take an inventory of his mental reactions to life, of his inward emotional states, of his faiths, fears, beliefs and hopes, he would be surprised to see how exactly they dovetail with his outward circumstances.

Circumstances do not create themselves; they are always molded by someone's thought patterns. In the collective life they are molded by the sum-total of all persons' thoughts; in our individual lives they are molded by our own personal reactions.

We cannot doubt that there is an Intelligence in the universe, which can mold our affairs into shapes of harmony. How should we proceed consciously to align ourselves with this larger possibility? First we should recognize that such a Power exists. Realizing that all energies, including mental and spiritual ones, operate according to Law, we should next attempt to discover how this Law operates, and then we should so use this Law that it will produce success instead of failure. The law of electricity will become our servant when we properly use it. So will any other law in nature. In dealing with the Laws of Mind and Spirit, we are dealing with natural laws.

The Law of Mind and Spirit responds to us by corresponding with our mental attitudes. That is, It operates for us through our belief. This is why we are told to have implicit confidence in It; to put our whole trust and faith in It; to believe sincerely, enthusiastically and joyfully that It will respond to us. This is the essence of faith.

Faith is a power which every man has but which few people use consciously. One man does not possess this power above another or to a greater degree. Everyone has the power, since everyone has consciousness. The question, then, is not do we have the power? It is merely, are we using it?

The Law which now holds us in bondage is the very Law that can free us. Does not the same wind blow the boat onto the reef or safely into harbor? *'Tis the set of the sail and not the gale which determines the way it goes.* Job said, "The thing which I greatly feared is come upon me," and Jesus, with that clarity of vision which marks him as the great spiritual genius of the ages, exclaimed, "As thou hast believed so be it done unto thee." Belief is a mental attitude; faith is an exalted spiritual, mental attitude. It is a certain way of thinking.

Anyone can use this Law of Life. I am certain you wish to use It for yourself, and I know that we all have a deep and sincere desire to use It for others.

Through faith in the Invisible we may claim the good we desire for ourselves or others, and when our whole inner being is in harmony with that good, then it is that we shall kiss the lips of our desire.

The Law of Life is already in your mind. Your problem is to apply It to your everyday needs. Naturally, the Intelligence and the Law, which are God, are abundantly able to bring to you or to anyone, everything necessary to happiness, to health and to success. Whether you call these things spiritual or material makes no difference, for God is *in* everything and *through* everything, and God *is* everything.

The Power of Life within you is a spiritual power, able to bring to you permanent peace, increasing happiness and joy, and greater material abundance. Those things which have made man miserable and unhappy can be eliminated through the conscious use of this Power. God could not visit fear or hate or impoverishment upon us, because God must be just the opposite to all of these things. It is, then, really necessary that the world should have a new concept of God; a new idea must be born in the minds of men about the nature of God and their relationship to this Divine Creative Spirit.

The only thing that can bring this joy, peace and prosperity to the world, is a direct experience of the Invisible. We must sense the immediate presence of Life. With simplicity and directness we must sense that the Spirit is at the center of our own lives. We should also learn to recognize It at the center of other people and working in human affairs.

While it is true that God Power is always with us, it is not true that we have always realized Its presence. To realize this is to be able to make conscious use of It, to direct It, for ourselves and for others.

If you knew that the Creative Energy of the universe were at your disposal and that the same Power which made everything is flowing through you, would you not naturally feel that you possessed the "pearl of great price"? If you knew how to use this Power would you not feel that you were on the verge of a new experience, wonderful and limitless in its possibility? Would you not have a new hope and enthusiasm about living?

The acceptance of the Power is only the first step toward Its use. For instance, people knew that electric energy existed long before it was very widely used. It was only as they gradually worked out methods for using this energy, for applying it to everyday purposes, that they were able to give to the world so many of the modern comforts which it now enjoys. Electric energy exists everywhere, it is present everywhere, it is available everywhere. We merely catch it and transform it into the particular kind of energy we desire. We direct it for definite purposes. In one place it lights a building, in another it runs a street car, and in another it is heating an oven to bake bread.

The Power of the Law of Life also exists everywhere. It is not enough merely to recognize that It is there; we must make definite use of It. The use that we make of It is what we call the Science of Mind and Spirit.

Faith acts in accord with law. As Dr. Carrel, author of *Man the Unknown,* has pointed out, faith, without contradicting physical laws, transcends them. Therefore, in using affirmations and denials, we must be sure that we generate faith.

Here is where faith plays such an important role in your work. You must have complete conviction in the reality of your word, in the way you use it, in the Law that is going to operate upon it, and in the result which this Principle is going to produce. You must have definite, concrete and specific faith. You must believe that the things you desire you now have.

Be sure that this is firmly fixed in your mind:

> *Faith lays hold of a Power which actually exists, and uses a Law which actually exists.*
> *Faith, through this Power and by this Law, causes the formless to take definite form.*
> *Faith is substance as well as power, and causes the good you have accepted to come into your experience.*

Everything you desire already exists as a possibility in Life. By accepting your desire as though it were already an established fact, you use the Law of this Principle in a way which causes It to bring into your experience the thing which you have definitely specified through your act of faith. There is a law of faith just as there is a law of gravity. Your faith can bring anything to you within the realm of your ability to conceive of such a thing.

This is not merely a blind faith; it is not a psychological, wishful thinking or wistful wishing; it is definite and deliberate. You know exactly what you are doing, just as definitely as you would know if you were planting a garden.

*The creative soil of thought is the mental medium through which this Law operates.*
*The idea is the seed.*
*Faith is the expectancy of fulfillment.*
*The result is the harvest.*

The seed time and harvest of your thought will depend entirely upon planting your affirmations with complete, unqualified faith, and then permitting the Principle to produce the harvest.

Think of Mind as a mental garden into which you may consciously put seeds of thought. You can consciously remove any of the plants which you have already planted either in ignorance or through fear. If one kind of thought produces a certain result, it follows that an opposite type of thought will produce an opposite result.

When you examine your thought, you will find it is made up of contradicting beliefs. In one moment you may be filled with faith, with enthusiasm for life, and the next moment a sense of depression may sweep over you. This shows that the thought patterns oppose each other. Mental instability and uncertainty follow. Your job is to clarify this whole field of thought and to learn to live affirmatively. Make a daily habit of using the following affirmations:

> *I am surrounded by an Infinite Intelligence which reacts to my thought.*
>
> *I realize that the creative power of this Divine Intelligence is with me now, and I know that I am using this Power and that my word, operating through It, will cause It to bring into my experience the good which I desire. (Mention some specific good and accept it as an already established fact.)*
>
> *Believing in divine guidance, I know that my mind is continuously impressed with the images of right action.*
>
> *I know that everything in my life is controlled by the action of Truth and Love.*
>
> *I am led, guided and inspired by the living Spirit.*
>
> *I am compelled to move in the right direction, always to know what to do and how to do it.*

> *I know that inwardly I am spiritually per-*
> *fect, I have complete happiness, and I ex-*
> *perience an abundance of good. Happi-*
> *ness and success rightfully belong to me.*
> *I am successful in all my undertakings.*
> *(Again consciously accept the good you*
> *desire.)*

Such statements as these tend to create faith. At first doubts and fears may float to the surface. Brush them aside and reassure yourself that you are dealing with absolute certainty.

> *Everyone who has had faith has demon-*
> *strated this Law.*
> *You are going to demonstrate It deliberately*
> *because you understand It.*
> *If you have not the required faith today, you*
> *are going to cultivate it; you are going to*
> *generate it.*
> *You are going to create the mental condi-*
> *tions which make possible the manifesta-*
> *tion of your desire.*

Your faith passes from blind belief into a thing of certainty. This is what constitutes perfect faith. Practice will make perfect, and you will soon discover that these things are true because you will be proving them.

Understanding the law of faith, and using it consciously, causes you to become the arbiter of your own fate. This is exactly what you desire. You are surrounded by a Power which is invisible. You may call this *God*, the *Creative Cause*, the *Invisible Principle*, the *Divine Mind* (as the Platonists, the ancient Greek philosophers, called it), the *Universal Mind*, or the *Great Truth*. We have decided to call It *Life*. It is the invisible Substance which gives rise to every form. It is always waiting to come forth into visible manifestation. It is unlimited, the Source of everything, the Cause of everything, and the Substance of everything.

Who would ever have thought that nylon stockings could be made by combining air, water and coal? Can you believe that if you combine thoughts of faith, hope and expectancy, success can come out of them? This means that when you have faith that something is going to happen, you are, in a sense, creating the very law which compels it to happen. This is not an act of the will or of concentration. It is a deep, silent, meditative belief; an inward, calm sense of expectancy; an unconfused acceptance.

The thought must be held firmly in place in order that the image which it reflects may not be distorted. Have you ever noticed your reflection in a pool of water, how distorted it looks if you move around? So it is with our thought world. We must hold it steady. We can bring our good almost to the surface and then, by denying it, cause it to recede from us.

We must accept the Spirit as our friend and the Law as our servant. The Spirit, which is the Mind that conceives everything, is now continuing Its creative act through us. Therefore, when a legitimate desire rises in our consciousness, it is a guarantee of its own fulfillment, provided we accept that fulfillment. This is the method Jesus taught:

*Our Father* . . . This suggests a universal sonship as well as a universal Fatherhood, Spirit or Parent Mind. This universal sonship is referred to as Christ in us. As there is but One Father, so there is but One Son. This Divine Incarnation is not something *separate from* our being, but is the very essence of that being. It is "Immanuel" or "God with us." *Our Father* is both immanent or indwelling, and transcendent or overdwelling. It is with this indwelling and overdwelling Presence that we commune.

. . . *which art* . . . This is a statement of absolute being. It implies that which Is, or the Truth of Being, the Absolute Cause, containing within Itself the potentiality of all effect. As universal, It is God, the Supreme Person; as individual, It is Christ in us, the incarnation of God.

. . . *in heaven.* The kingdom of heaven is within. The creative power of Spirit exists at the center of our own being—in heaven, in harmony, in all of Its fullness. There is nothing static in Life.

*Our Father which art in heaven* is ever flowing through us, giving birth to new personal experiences.

*Hallowed be thy name.* In the exultation of his "jubilant and beholding soul," Jesus proclaimed the wondrous name of God, the ineffable sweetness of the Divine Nature and the glory of Its eternal reign. "Hallowed be thy name" is more than a salutation, it is a song of praise. It is, "Holy, holy, holy, Lord God Almighty."

*Thy kingdom come.* The kingdom of God is joy. The kingdom of God is harmony and wholeness. It is completion, perfection and peace. It is that to which *nothing need be added* and from which *nothing can be taken.* The highest treasure of this kingdom is love.

*Thy will be done . . .* Reason tells us that the will of God must be consistent with the nature of the Divine Being, hence if God's nature is peace, then God's will must be peace. If God is Life, then the will of God is Life. If God is love and happiness, the will of God also must be love and happiness.

*. . . in earth, as it is in heaven.* It is said that one of the disciples of Jesus asked him when the kingdom of heaven would come on earth and he answered, "When the without shall become as the within." Plato, several hundred years before Jesus, had also taught that the kingdom of heaven is within. He said that our external world,

including our physical bodies, is a gross image or manifestation of this inner kingdom. Plato believed in a divine prototype or spiritual reality within all manifest form. Therefore, he said that when the image turns to its prototype its labors will cease and it will come to its journey's end, because it will discover that the without and the within are really one.

This concept of an inner perfection really runs through much of our modern psychological teaching which, almost unwittingly, is based upon the supposition that there is an inner principle of perfection, that nature is already complete and that if we could restore our emotional reactions to the equilibrium of nature we should reintegrate the personality. That is, it would be made whole. This sheds a new light on this remarkable saying of Jesus when he told us to be perfect without even as we are already perfect within. "Be ye therefore perfect, even as your Father which is in heaven is perfect." *Thy kingdom come, Thy will be done in earth as it is in heaven.* The broad scope of this revelation of Jesus includes man, with his physical body and his physical environment, as some part of the divine pattern. It announces that God is all there is; Life is perfect; Its freedom and joy are available. Wholeness is not something we create, but discover.

*Give us* . . . Browning said, " 'Tis Thou, God, who

63

givest; 'tis I who receive." As manna from heaven, the Divine Bounty supplies our human needs when the Divine Will is complied with. It is the nature of the Divine to give, it is the nature of man to receive—not some of the gifts of life, but all of them. *The Father which art* holds within Himself all the gifts of life, peace, joy, happiness, eternal and ever-increasing self-expression. We are not asked to be less, but ever more, ourselves. The Divine Givingness is the eternal and inexhaustible gift of heaven. This gift consciously must be received. Our fears, lacks, limitations, worries, pathetically suggest how inadequate our receiving has been. To fulfill the Divine Givingness we must set up an equal receivingness.

. . . *this day* . . . NOW, today, this moment, this present time in which we are living.

. . . *our daily bread.* Our daily bread means whatever we need, whenever we need it, wherever we need it, and for as long as we need it.

*And forgive us our debts* . . . Spirit is not only the Giver, It is the Forgiver. When we come into the light we are in the light and in that light there is no darkness. So Jesus taught that as we turn to God He turns to us. The father did not condemn the prodigal upon his return, but embraced him. The Eternal Nature is love and givingness, thus Jesus said that to him who loves much, much is forgiven, which explains the next clause:

... *as we forgive our debtors.* The action between the Universal and the individual is reciprocal. The Universal turns to us as we turn to It. What is this but an illustration that man's own thought and act condemn him and that his own thought and act release him from such condemnation according to the law of cause and effect. "There is no sin but a mistake and no punishment but a consequence." *Forgive us our debts, as we forgive our debtors,* perhaps one of the greatest phrases in sacred literature, places immediate salvation within the reach of all, but automatically causes us to suffer so long as we impose suffering. We could not ask for a more complete justice, a greater givingness, nor a more exalted concept of the Divine Forgivingness. The nature of God is revealed as infinite tenderness coupled with exact law.

*And lead us not into temptation* . . . This is not so much a supplication as it is a statement of spiritual conviction. Spirit cannot lead man into temptation.

... *but deliver us from evil.* The Divine Nature does not lead us into temptation but delivers us from evil. Just as light delivers us from darkness.

*For thine is the kingdom, and the power, and the glory, forever and ever. Amen.* This kingdom, this power and this glory never change. The Truth is forever established. Eternal in Its infancy, eternal in Its maturity, It knows no decay.

Even though Life has already provided for our good, we must accept that good. Our acceptance should be more definite. Therefore, we must make some kind of a demand upon the Power. If you went into a grocery store and were looking for a can of corn, you would not stare blindly at a clerk back of the counter and just sort of mumble the word "groceries." You would step briskly up to him and say, "Give me a can of corn, please." And he would hand you a can of corn, not something else. He would not give you a cake of soap or a package of cornflakes. This grocery clerk represents the tiniest fraction of the Intelligence of the Principle which responds to you.

Do you think it reasonable to suppose that this Life could respond to you other than by doing so through the act of corresponding to your thought? Your image of thought is the mold, and, in a sense, your faith is the substance dropped into this mold, or, perhaps it would be better to say, it is the avenue through which the substance is pushed out into your experience. This means that when you ask for something you really receive it through the act of believing that you already possess what you have asked for.

Asking and receiving are merely two ends of one law. When you ask for something, that is, when you affirm the presence of your desire (for this is the most effective method of asking), you should believe that this desire is already an accomplished fact, it is taking form on the invisible plane. And if you have absolute faith and conviction that this is the truth, then you will be certain to experience the result of your desire.

The Law of Life is a law of goodness and if you use It in any harmful way, your use of It will hurt you. This is the only limitation the Law seems to have, and it is not a limitation at all. Rather, it is complete protection. But if there is no malice in your heart toward anyone; if you are permitting love to emanate from you, and good will toward all; if you sincerely desire the good of all, please remember you have every right to include yourself. You are the one person living who is intimately acquainted with yourself. You are the one to whom yourself is the most important. This is not self-conceit, it is logical self-justification.

You exist that this Power may have another, a unique, outlet for Its expression. The more life you express, the more of It flows through you. Therefore, every legitimate desire you have is the pushing of this Power through you into Its own self-expression. In this way you are in partnership with the Infinite.

# Chapter VII

Y OU DO NOT have to grow old. It is now psychologically demonstrated that the mind does not grow old. We are just as young mentally at ninety as we were at nine. It is now scientifically demonstrated, according to some of the world's leading physicists, that our physical body renews itself each year. It is now scientifically demonstrated that love may rise triumphant over hate. It is now scientifically demonstrated that most of our physical ailments are results of a negative use of the Power that is within us. It is now scientifically demonstrated that at least a large portion of our accidents are unconsciously invited.

You are all familiar with these findings and it is unnecessary to elaborate on them, but it is important that we should analyze their meaning:

*The mind cannot grow old because there is only One Mind which we all use. This Mind was not born and will never die; It is eternal.*

*The reason why the physical body is not yet a year old and never will be, is that the continuous activity of the Mind Principle in us is forever dissolving and forever reforming the body.*

*The reason why so many of our accidents and diseases are now considered results of psychological causes, is that the only activity there is in us and around us is the activity of Mind through us. That is, the activity of this Life through our thought.*

The mind does not grow old. Well, what is the mind anyway? There you have me, for I have not the slightest idea what the mind is. I had a friend who once had the great privilege of meeting Mr. Thomas Edison, and in a burst of enthusiasm she asked, "Mr. Edison, what is electricity?" He looked at her very kindly and with a sort of whimsical smile answered, "My dear, electricity *is*, use it." This great inventive genius knew more about electricity than most, but he did not claim to know what it is. As a matter of fact, electricity is an energy in the universe which we use. You did not make it, I did not make it—perhaps even God did not create electrical energy. Probably it has always existed. But you will say, "What has this to do with my mind growing old?" Nothing in particular, except that it should help us to understand that the energies of nature, whether we call them electricity or the energy of creative imagination, belong to Life, and your mind is some part of this Reality.

The real power of thought, of decision and imagination never grows old. We used to be told that our mental capacities reached their highest peak around the age of twenty-five or thirty. Now we are told that while our mental powers do not seem to work quite as rapidly as we grow older, they do work more accurately. This means that your real mental power never declines. Perhaps you could say of it as you do of Life Itself, that it is the same yesterday, today and forever.

Did you ever ask yourself the question, "What is this illusive thing I call my mind anyway?" Did you ever try to weigh and measure thought, imagination or will? This would be impossible, would it not? Now modern science is telling us that the capacity to think, to imagine and to create is ageless, just as certain at ninety as at nine or nineteen or twenty-nine. Do you not think, if we could learn the real relationship between mind and body, that some day we should discover that even the body does not have to grow old?

There was a time in human history when the life expectancy was not over twenty years. Now the average has increased to more than sixty-two years for men and sixty-four years for women, and the horizon of human expectancy is ever being pushed farther away. How do you and I know but that the time may come when people will live to be hundreds of years old?

If the mind never grows old, and if it is the mind that really dominates the body, why should we not expect both mind and body some day to remain almost indefinitely on this planet? Well, probably that is a long way off, and I do not think it matters much anyway. The thing that really matters is that while you and I are living in this world we should be one hundred per cent alive, filled with joy and enthusiasm, filled with energy and power.

Our trouble is not that the mind grows old, but that we let it slow down. We begin to feel that we are getting older, and mentally accept the belief that the vitality of youth is no longer with us. Now, certain experiments, made by eminent psychologists, have proved that the older man, provided he does not lose self-confidence, is more valuable than the younger one, both to himself and to others. Naturally you would expect to find this, would you not, for the older man has a wealth of experience back of him, and, even though his mental processes may have slowed down somewhat, according to the tests made they are more accurate. After all, perhaps we are in too much of a hurry. It is better to be accurate than speedy. But even the slowing down process is not very perceptible. Our main trouble is a lack of the will to imagine ourselves as always young.

After a certain number of years we are likely to get into a rut. Accepting the false belief that one is getting old causes the creative imagination to act as though he were old. If we are some part of Life how can we grow old unless God also grows old? Michaelangelo was made superintending architect of St. Peters when he was seventy-two. At ninety-two he said he was still learning.

One of our greatest psychologists says that it is a mistake to believe in "the time honored doctrine that childhood is the period in which one learns most readily to read, write, speak and understand a language." In an investigation conducted some years ago by a Chicago physician, in which he investigated the lives of four hundred of the most outstanding men and women who ever lived, he discovered that their greatest achievements were accomplished at the average age of fifty, and that many of them did their best work after they were seventy or eighty.

If we take this basic idea that the mind never grows old and that any apparent mental age is merely the result of not using the mind, then I think we shall begin to experience a real resurrection here and now.

Would you really like to stay young forever? Then stop thinking old thoughts. Learn to revitalize your mental processes. Every morning when you awake, say:

*Today I am going to be enthusiastic.*
*Today I am going keenly to enjoy everything*
*I do.*
*My mind is at an eternal springtime.*

Perhaps you will be surprised at the physical wrinkles this new thought will erase, for "Soul is form and doth the body make."

If you learn to keep your thought fresh and young, invigorated with enthusiasm and filled with hope; if you have a keen enthusiastic zest for living, you never can grow old. Let us stop looking forward to old age and learn to look forward to eternal youth.

Why not start today to resurrect the hopes and aspirations which you have laid on the shelf? Get them down and dust them off; shake them loose from their tomb, from the burial robes in which you have so carefully laid them out. Let the dream of youth return; let the enthusiastic ardor for living revitalize every part of your being.

Let us stop thinking about dying, or quitting, or getting through with living, and let us learn to enjoy and appreciate the eternal here and the everlasting now. Let us allow all the hope and enthusiasm, which we once thought had died, to come to life again. Won't it be wonderful to be consciously present at our own resurrection! Just as Jesus stood at the tomb of Lazarus and in a loud voice cried, "Lazarus come forth!" let us stand before the tomb of our dead selves and with all the imagination, will and feeling we have, say, "Come forth and live again!"

You see, the whole thing ties together and provides the most glorious concept ever delivered to the mind of man: the concept of yourself as master through the conscious use of the Power which you have been using unconsciously.

Could you ask for anything better than this? And don't you think that, having discovered such a Mind Principle, the next step to take is to learn how to so use this Power, for yourself and others, that It will never produce anything other than a blessing? To so use It that It will produce health instead of disease; wealth instead of poverty; happiness instead of misery; clarity instead of confusion; life instead of death?

In the remaining chapters of this book we shall learn how to use this Power consciously and intelligently both for ourselves and for others. We are going to be very humble in this, but with no sense of false humility—humble as we stand in awe before the tremendous possibilities before us, while, at the same time, radiant with expectancy as we contemplate the possibility of the blessings in store for ourselves and others.

We are going to take a truly scientific attitude in that we shall view this Power as Absolute Law. We are also going to take a truly spiritual attitude because we know that only through love can there be a perfect fulfillment of the Law of Life. We are going to learn how to combine our word with the Law of Life in such a manner that new and limitless possibilities will open up before us. We should do this with joy and enthusiasm, for joy and enthusiasm are the very essence of life.

We have been re-examining our previous beliefs in the light of a new understanding. And we have every right to expect that our world, in the light of this new understanding, shall take on an aura of warmth and color, of happiness and satisfaction, of gratification and accomplishment, which our old world lacked. And we should believe that we are destined to take part in a new faith in God which shall no longer see as through a glass quite so darkly, but, open-faced, shall more completely sense that divine benediction after which endless ages have sought— peace on earth and good will among man.

## Chapter VIII

I N STUDYING the words of Jesus we find that he never talked much about the negative conditions he wished to change. He took an opposite position. Instead of telling God how sick and poor people were, how famished and lonely they were, he affirmed the exact opposite. He told the lame to walk, the blind to see, the dumb to speak and the deaf to hear. He commanded the waves to be still, even while they were turbulently tossing themselves around him. He was calm in the midst of the storm.

When you pray or affirm your good, close the door of your consciousness to everything which denies this good and state your needs, not as a supplication but as an affirmation of acceptance. Spiritual mind treatment is a recognition that our good is at hand; an affirmation that we are now experiencing this good. We shall not gain happiness by continuing to repeat mental patterns of unhappiness. We cannot enter into the joy of living while we remain sad.

The thing simmers itself down to this. Can we, in the midst of negative conditions, accept a greater good? If we can we shall be complying with the Law of Life. We shall be giving Life a chance to work for us.

Suppose every day you say to yourself:

*My thoughts are radiant with the Light of Spirit.*
*There is no darkness in my mind.*
*I am directed by the Spirit of Wisdom.*
*I am guided into right action, into happiness and success, because the Light of Spirit shines from the very center of my being.*
*This Light illumines my path and makes straight the way before me.*
*This Light is God, the living Spirit Almighty.*

We are to come to Life, not dragging our burdens and woes to hurl into the face of the Infinite, but gently we are to lay them down at the altar of our faith as we turn from the valley of our previous despair. As we make our ascent from appearance to Reality, there is to be a song on our lips and joy in our heart. The Light of the Spirit of Life shines from the center of the soul. It is a beam of the Eternal Radiance. In the Light there is no darkness. In that Light shall we see the light.

The main impulsion of Life is Love. Plato said It is love, beauty and wisdom. Life is more than law, It is also pure Spirit. What we need, in addition to the knowledge that a power flows through us and operates upon our thought with mathematical precision, is to realize that the greatest use of this Power comes from more completely surrendering ourselves to Its love.

Remember that the Power *in* you *is* you; It is Itself *as* you. The more you live, the more completely It is expressed through you. The self-surrender necessary for a more complete outlet to this Power is not a surrender of the individuality or of the true Self. It is merely a surrender of the false self to the true Self.

The following will help you to see exactly how this worked with an English architect who had come to America to regain his health. His had been a complete breakdown; nerves shattered, digestive organs out of repair; insomnia, coupled with terrific fear. I never knew how he happened to stumble into one of my noon lectures in downtown Los Angeles, nor what caused him to spend a few weeks in a small private sanitarium, which I conducted at that time, in a suburb of Los Angeles. But, there he was riding home with me one evening, and, of course, unfolding his tale of woe.

A gentleman, a scholar, and a truly great artist, he had designed some of the finest buildings in London, and yet here he was thousands of miles from home, distraught, almost insane. His fear was pathetic. He clung to me like a child, imploring relief, begging for a few moments of peace.

Fortunately, I was able to uncover his trouble and bring to the light of day the emotional state which was gnawing at the very center of his life. As in most cases, he had not the slightest conscious knowledge of what caused his trouble. He had just finished erecting a very large and important public building in London, and, of course, his thought was that the strain had "done him in," as the English say. But I knew better, just as any psychologist or metaphysician would have known. I proceeded to get at the root of his trouble. This was not easy, but finally we did uncover the cause of his distress. *He hated his older brother.* But he was not conscious of this inner hatred which was gnawing at the vitals of his being. It came out, however, in the recitation of his life's history.

Being a cultured and kindly man, Mr. A . . . would never permit any thought of hate to rise to the level of his conscious mind. That thing which some psychologists call "the censor," which technically may be defined as a mental agency within the mind, preventing depressing or painful memories, thoughts or impulses from arising into consciousness—yes, this is what "the censor" really means—this censor, or mental mechanism, that did not wish him to be shocked by the realization that he hated his brother, just covered that hatred up and there it rankled. He thought he had both forgiven and forgotten, when, as a matter of fact, subconsciously he had neither forgiven nor forgotten. This painful memory rankling at the very center of his psyche had already destroyed his health and was about to ravage his mentality.

Finally, when the whole story came out, I was able to show him the real cause of his trouble. He not only forgave, he was able to forget in the sense that his memory no longer tormented him. He found an inward peace and in a few weeks he went on his way rejoicing.

What power lies in conscious forgiving! Peace rises from the depths of one's being when confusion, hate and resentment are dissolved.

Hate was what this man surrendered. *We never have to surrender anything that really belongs to Life; we surrender only that which is opposed to It.*

Take time frequently to become still in your thought and let the barriers of your personality slip away into space. Think of yourself as one with the whole. At first you will feel a sense of separation, then gradually there will come a sense of being merged with something bigger, something more universal. You will not be less yourself, you will be more, infinitely more, yourself. Try to feel that there is no barrier between you and It.

In those moments when you let go of all restriction, of all sense of limitation, consciously using your word for definite purposes, you will discover a hidden power of which you have never dreamed.

Life is the Giver of everything. It is, in a sense, both the Giver and the gift. It is both Itself and you. This Life is a perfect unit. Therefore, there is nothing between It and you other than your sense of separation from It. The knowledge of this is what King Solomon referred to when he said, "With all thy getting get understanding." "She is more precious than rubies . . . Her ways are ways of pleasantness, and all her paths are peace. She is a tree of life to them that lay hold upon her."

Nothing is more important than that we should gain spiritual understanding. On the other hand, nothing is more important than that we should refuse to be confused over what is often meant by spiritual understanding.

The Spirit in which we live, move and have our being also lives, moves and has some part of Its being in us. We are individualizations, personifications of It; centers of consciousness in It. To understand this is the inner secret, "the pearl of great price." To unify with Life, to get in tune with the Infinite, is every man's search, whether or not he is conscious of the fact.

Think these things out carefully, with the utmost simplicity, until you see that you could not move a finger if it were not for Life. You could not think a thought if it were not for the intelligence of Life. You could not exist without It because It is you. Since this is so, you will never cease to exist—you will always be more and never less yourself.

Every right recognition you give to this Life will increase your own livingness. Every time you use It in a dynamic way you will be cultivating the ability to use It in an even more effective manner, and this will go on forever. There will never come a time when this unfoldment will cease.

Let me tell you about a man who was so unfortunate as to have become an alcoholic addict. This incident happened in a San Francisco hotel. Mr. Armor, one of our teachers at the Institute of Religious Science in Los Angeles, and I were visiting that wonderful city. What was my surprise, one evening, to receive a telephone call from another room in the same hotel and to hear a familiar voice, but rather a groggy one, say, "Hello, can you come over to room . . . for a few moments?"

A moment later I was knocking at his door. There he lay sprawled out on the bed, and I was greeted with these words: "I'm drunk."

"You are the first person," I replied, "I have ever known who claimed to be drunk while appearing to be perfectly sober. What are you lying on the bed for? Why don't you get up?"

"I can't stand up," was his reply. "That is one of the funny things about my drinking—I can get so drunk that I can neither stand nor walk, but I never lose consciousness. Which makes it just that much worse."

"Even though your body is drunk," I remarked,

82

"your mind is perfectly clear. Why don't you stop drinking? Sober up and go home."

"Ah, that's just the trouble," he said, "I can't. This sometimes goes on for weeks."

"And do you always go off by yourself like this?" I asked.

"Yes," he replied. "I am a lone drinker. I don't know why I do it. Something beyond my control impels me. What, in the name of God, is my trouble? Can you help me?"

Imagine sitting on the edge of a bed talking to a man whose mentality seemed as clear as anyone's could be, and yet so drunk he couldn't stand alone!

"But what do you do when you find yourself in this condition?" I asked.

"Usually," he replied, "after a week or two I send for my wife. She generally is able to bring me out of it. But, somehow, I thought you might do this for me."

"And just what do you think I can do for you?" I inquired.

"Oh," he said, "you know, I really believe in your stuff and I think I have some understanding of it. Surely there is some power that can help me."

What a tragedy! I thought. A successful professional man overcome by a habit which, while in his particular case was not able to reduce him to insensibility, still had him cornered, as it were, beaten, defeated.

"Would you really like to give up this stuff for good?" I asked.

"That is the one prayer of my life," he said. "I have as fine a wife as ever lived and two beautiful children. It is because of them that I go away when this thing takes possession of me. After a while I wire for my wife."

My next question was to the point: "Are you sure that you wish to give up this habit for good?"

"How can you ask such a question," he said, "when you see me in this condition? Even now," he continued, "my craving is irresistible."

Perhaps you will be surprised at what we did next. We sent down to the bar for a bottle of whiskey. It is well known to those familiar with this subject, whether we call them psychologists or metaphysicians, that habits are not successfully treated through will power. Something different from mere mental determination must happen to the emotional nature of an alcoholic or drug addict, if he is to be free from the bonds which have clamped him into his mental prison. This is why we ordered the whiskey. I told him to drink all he wished. As a matter of fact, I placed the bottle, with a glass of water, at his bedside and left, telling him if this were not enough I would secure more for him during the evening or the night.

"But," he implored, "aren't you going to help me? Is anything going to happen? What are you going to do anyway? Shall I wire to Los Angeles for my wife?"

"No," I replied. "Mr. Armor and I are occupying rooms close to you. We will get busy and lick this thing, and we are going to do it tonight."

I wanted to get away from him, away from seeing him in his defeated condition. I wished to get that mental image out of mind that I might see him strong, self-reliant, poised in pure Spirit, unshaken, unshakable.

It was early in the evening. We had just had dinner. I returned to my room and said to Mr. Armor, "Too bad, we won't be going anywhere tonight. We have a job to do. Mr. B . . . is across the hall, drunk. He wants to be healed and we are going to do it right now."

Perhaps you will be interested to know just how we went about our work. We made ourselves comfortable, relaxed. First one and then the other took up this thought for him: "This man is conscious that he is pure Spirit. He is poised and at peace within himself. There is nothing in him that craves alcohol. He is not seeking to escape from anything. He meets every issue of life without fear. There is nothing to run away from. Nothing to avoid. At all times he has a sense of well-being, of happiness, of security and of self-expression. There is no memory of ever having received any pleasure or benefit from alcohol. There is no anticipation that he ever can receive pleasure or benefit from it. The Spirit within him is satisfied. It is radiant. It never seeks to escape from Itself. It exists

85

in Its own sense of self-adequacy. It exists in joy, in freedom and in peace."

We did our work orally. First Mr. Armor would work for ten or fifteen minutes, then I would take up the thought and continue, each speaking aloud. We worked for several hours until somehow, in a way which no one completely understands, hence which no one can perfectly explain, we both seemed to have a sense of release for our friend. We seemed to feel that what we had said about him was true; that there really was no intoxicated man. There was only a glorious sense of divine sonship, free from fear, perfectly contented, happy and radiant, self-assured, united with the Infinite and one with complete satisfaction.

Early the next morning the phone rang and a steady, cheerful voice said, "Can you come over to my room for a moment?"

I was there almost immediately. He was relaxed, calm and as sober as he had ever been in his life. His first remark was, "You will find the rest of that stuff in the closet."

There it was, all but about two drinks that he had taken. He never took another drink—he never had the desire.

You see, we were using the Law of Life for a definite purpose. There is no mystery about this. Anyone using the same method would have had the same result.

There is a principle involved in all this, the principle which the Science of Mind teaches. Naturally, if there is such a principle, then there must be a definite method of using it. For instance, there is a principle of electricity and there is a science of electricity. The science of electricity is the technique or the method for using the principle. The recognition of a principle is but the first step toward the use of it.

Just as we are surrounded by electric energy which we generate and use for definite purposes, so we are surrounded by a Creative Mind which we also may use for definite purposes. We all know that there are certain physical appliances which we use in generating electricity. We call them distributors, transformers, etc. We realize that these mechanical appliances must be used if we are to catch power from the waterfall, the barrel of oil, or the bin of coal. There also are appliances we must use for catching the Power of Life. But the appliances we use in the Science of Mind are thoughts and ideas—these are the instruments.

We have, then, mental generators, mental distributors, etc. Can't you see that this is really what is behind faith and prayer? Jesus very definitely taught that the world in which we live is a world of mind and manifestation; he told us that thoughts are things. Faith, belief and conviction lay hold of an invisible Power which we can use.

Crying out to Life, beseeching It to be good, has no effect whatsoever upon It; It already is good. Asking It to give you life produces no good results; It has already incarnated Itself in you, as you. But inward awareness unifies the intellect with Life and binds the personal man back to the Universal Presence. This is what is meant by spiritual understanding and realization.

If the gift of Life is already made, then our part must be to accept, receive, believe in and use it. Life has endowed our thought with creativeness. Through ignorance we have brought about the very disasters we seek emancipation from. What then should we do? We should reverse the process. Just what does this actually mean? It means that we should carefully watch our thought world, straighten it out, correct it, re-educate it, until finally the subjective reactions of our thought (the automatic, mechanical and habitual reactions of our thought) pass from a negative into an affirmative state.

The Law of Life operates upon the images of your thought. If your thought is restricted and unhappy, you will be causing It to create restricting and unhappy circumstances. Only a two inch stream of water can flow through a two inch pipe. A gallon measure will hold but four quarts. This would be true even though you dipped your measure into the ocean. You are not limiting the ocean nor causing it to be evil because you dip up four quarts instead of a barrel. The ocean has no desire to limit you. In a personal sense, it can only give you what you take, for your taking is its givingness in the form of your taking. This is one of the greatest lessons of life. "It is done unto you as you believe."

The Law of Life is like a mirror. It reflects back to you the images of your thoughts in exactly the way you think them. You cannot say that It is little or that It gives you but a small portion of Itself when your own thought patterns are limiting this gift. Life has already delivered everything It has to you. But in your personal experience even that which It has given must, of a necessity, be limited to that which you take.

It is, then, of greatest value to learn how to receive more abundantly. Just as one studying the piano patiently goes over his lesson until finally his action becomes automatic, so in using the Life Principle you must be patient with yourself. You must learn to strike the right chord. The right chord is always one of harmony.

*Learn to receive more by daily practicing the Presence of Abundance.*

*Learn to use the Law of Life in a more expansive manner by daily practicing belief in It.*

At first this may sound strange because probably you will say, "I already believe in It." Remember, your belief in It is perhaps somewhat limited by your experience. And so—

*You are practicing a greater expectation.*

*You are believing in more and accepting more.*

*You are opening every channel of your mind to a larger influx.*

The following is a simple practice which may greatly benefit you:

*The One Supreme Power, Life, Intelligence and Spirit is within, around and through me. My word is the activity of this Infinite Mind and is the law of good in my experience.*

*It is perfect in its action and permanent in its manifestation. Infinite Intelligence governs, sustains and animates me. Good alone goes from me and good alone returns to me.*

*The Law of Spirit establishes harmony and right adjustment of all personal, family and business affairs or conditions in my life. I am supplied with every good thing. I am happy, radiant and complete. The Source of all life manifests as peace, harmony and wholeness in my experience.*

*Everything that I do, say or think is governed by pure Intelligence and inspired by Divine Wisdom. I am guided into right action. I am surrounded with friendship, love and beauty. Enthusiastic joy, vitality and inspiration are in everything I do.*

*I represent that Life which cannot want, which is forever manifesting freedom, self-expression and wholeness. I represent the principle of Divine Activity which never tires, which is birthless, changeless and deathless. I am receptive to the inexhaustible energy of the universe, to Divine Guidance and to the influx of perfect life, perfect ideas, and complete joy.*

*I know as a result of this spiritual realization, happiness, health and prosperity immediately will spring into action and manifest in everything I do, say or think.*

*I am conscious of Divine Guidance, of complete happiness, abundant health and increasing prosperity. I am aware of my partnership with the Infinite. I know that everything I do shall prosper.*

*I accept this word. I know that it is the Presence, the Power and the Activity of God in me. I know I am conscious of Divine Guidance, of inward peace and poise. I immediately become conscious of a more abundant life. I expect greater good, more happiness and a complete success in every constructive thing which I undertake.*

*Again I affirm that this word, being the presence of the Spirit in me, is the Law of God*

> *operating through me, and establishing in*
> *me that which is good, beautiful and true.*
> *It is done. I accept. I believe. I know.*

Don't be discouraged if it takes a little time to gain the inner understanding you desire. The time you spend will be more than worth while.

> *Your first step is to come to a more complete*
> *realization of who and what you are.*
> *Your next step is to enter into a more definite*
> *understanding of your relationship with*
> *the Power.*
> *Your final step is to use the Power for your-*
> *self and others.*
> *Start at once affirming your God given do-*
> *minion over anything which contradicts*
> *the nature of Life.*
> *Rearrange your thought to conform to the*
> *belief that you are one with all the Power*
> *and all the Presence there is; It is flowing*
> *through you as health, happiness and suc-*
> *cess.*
> *Bless everything you do; take the restric-*
> *tions off your efforts and announce them*
> *to be prosperous, good and perfect.*
> *Know that the Power is flowing through you*
> *creatively in the direction which your at-*
> *tention gives to It.*
> *Begin right where you are. Don't wait until*

*you get an understanding as big as a
house or as broad as an ocean or as deep
as a well.*

If you have grasped the simple truth that a positive statement can neutralize a negative one, then begin by making the positive statement in simplicity and complete faith. Abandon yourself to a complete faith in the Power. Don't argue with anyone about this. Don't listen to anything which contradicts it. This is keeping your eye single to the Power.

Remember, It is not some power; It is All Power. It made everything. It made what we call big and little. It knows no difference between big and little. It does not know that a million dollars is more than a nickel. It does not know that to heal a cancer is any different from healing a wart on your finger. We are the ones who believe in limitation because we live in a sense of disunion with life.

*In joy go within yourself to meet this Life.
Expect It to respond.
Know that It is going to.
Have no anxiety.
Relax and trust—believe.
Don't deny It.
Begin with whatever affirmative and con-
    structive thinking you have and build on
    that.
Refuse to dwell in the darkness of unbelief.*

93

*Refuse to be overcome by negative sugges-
tions.*
*Boldly step through the place of doubt and
plant your feet on the solid rock of faith.*

If you are faithful in using these few simple
methods of procedure, you will be amazed at the
lightninglike speed with which the Power will reveal
Itself to you. In every way act as though It were real.
Practice the presence of this Power until It is real to
you. Don't think you have to put on a long face and
imagine that you look like Buddha or Plato.

*Life is enthusiastic joy.*
*It contains the great song of being.*
*There is nothing little, mean or petty about
It.*
*It is not browbeating you.*
*It is not beating you over the head with a
cosmic club.*
*It is not knocking you down on your knees
asking you to beseech light to be light or
truth to be truth.*

Inspiration and enthusiasm are necessary to the
highest use of this Power—quick joy in recognition
and gladness in realization. There is something triumphant and transcendent about it. Don't be afraid
of these higher emotions. Consciousness of the Power
will buoy you up, it will not pull you down.

94

*Don't let your thought stagnate.*

*Loose everything that is in you and expect a larger flow.*

*Keep every channel open, alive, awake and aware.*

*Live, think and act as though the entire nature of this Life were delivered to you individually.*

*Remember that the more you give the more greatly you will receive.*

# Chapter IX

THE GOOD things of life for which we seek are but echoes of the true self knocking at the door of consciousness. Everyone seeks an inward sense of certainty, without which happiness and satisfaction are impossible. We all seek an inner awareness of something greater than we are, something so complete that we can find completion in it, something so vast that we may anticipate exploring its nature through endless eternities.

Someone has said that the soul is homesick; that it cannot recover until it finds complete union with its Source. Intuitively we know that such a union with a Source of power must exist. If the pipe that conducts water from a high reservoir to our homes becomes disconnected, it does not mean that the water has dried up at its source. If the stream of electric energy flowing into our homes becomes disconnected, no light is delivered, though the universe be packed solid with electric energy.

So it is with our life. Its Source is an infinite sea of energy, of power, of love and of wisdom. That which connects the outward man with this Source is his inward life, those inward thoughts and feelings which make up his *consciousness*. This consciousness is two-fold. We have a conscious consciousness and a subconscious consciousness. The former constitutes the thoughts and movements of everyday life. Our subconscious is the sum-total of all our conscious states, plus the influence of inherited tendencies and the accumulated thought of the race mind.

This vast accumulation pushed back into the subconscious is what the psychologist deals with, for the whole problem of modern psychology is the subconscious. The philosophy underlying that branch of the Science of Mind, called the psychology of the unconscious, may be stated as follows:

There is an emotional craving toward self-expression, a feeling nature in everyone which demands outlet. This emotional craving some psychologists call the *libido*. The libido must have something upon which to discharge its emotional content. The early object of the libido is naturally the image of the parents or those upon whom the child depends for its gratification. The child identifies itself with this libido object and throughout life more or less unconsciously repeats the thought patterns which are first impressed upon its subconscious being.

If in infancy or early childhood the craving for self-gratification is frustrated, pushed back upon itself, the child receives a psychic, subjective or mental wound which remains unhealed. From the standpoint of a psychological analysis, a healing is brought about by bringing the unconscious reactions to the surface and causing them to be self-seen, to be understood. If this is accomplished, the repressed energy is dissipated and the psychic pressure is either lessened or entirely removed.

The psychological basis for the inner conflict, which exists in the minds of so many people, is largely a subconscious sense of having been rejected, of not being wanted, or of being unworthy. This creates an unconscious sense of guilt, of condemnation, and gives rise later in life to what is called the inferiority complex.

From a psychological viewpoint it is believed that most of our traumatic (that is, mental or emotional) shocks, date back to infancy or early childhood. (Of course, this unconscious sense of frustration in many instances is imaginary.) Some psychologists hold that repressions and unconscious shocks may be traced to any incident in life which gives one a sense of not being wanted or which creates any form of unconscious anxiety, such as economic insecurity, anxiety over the future, a lack of adaptability to circumstances, etc.

Any mental state of fear or anxiety, of frustration

or rejection, of condemnation or censure, may, in a sensitive person, produce a psychic wound which, festering inwardly, may create a disease. This is more than just imagination. Indeed, there is a psychic basis for the largest part of our physical troubles.

It is now known that a sustained mental sense of insecurity can produce indigestion, stomach ulcers, constipation and other internal disturbances. A sustained emotional tension can produce a hypertension which may become the background for many forms of heart ailment. A sustained sense of grief can also do this. Worry over the loss of a fortune can easily produce a fatal heart condition.

The early emotional atmosphere which surrounds the infant and the child, can so condition his unconscious that he may develop neurotic tendencies later in life.

I once treated a little boy, about ten years of age, who was sent home from school because of a severe throat affliction. He was told to have his tonsils removed and that he should wear glasses. This seemed so unnatural in a child who otherwise was perfectly normal that I inquired into the emotional atmosphere which surrounded him.

The parents were separated. Through a court decision the child was to be with his mother during the school week and with his father over weekends. It was the emotional conflict between the father and mother which caused his physical trouble. The mother did not wish him to see his father. Her emotional condition was reflected in him.

I explained this to her, told her to tell the child to go gladly, to assure him that it was a fine thing for him to be with his dad part of the time. I helped her to remove the emotional strain from her own mind, to clear her thought of sensitiveness and unhappiness because of the separation from her husband. In a very short time the child was perfectly normal.

It is now known that childhood bed wetting may often be attributed to an intolerable mental and emotional condition surrounding the child in the family life. This emotional condition probably takes the form of over-irritation and agitation, of mental combat and conflict.

These cases help us better to understand the action of the unconscious thought upon the physical body. Mental hygiene is just as real as physical hygiene, and equally necessary. To be well one must be happy. To be happy one must have a sense of security. One must have confidence in himself, in those around him and in the universe itself. He must be unified with himself and with life.

Since our earliest emotional reactions are those of infancy and childhood, we are all subjectively conditioned early in life. We learn either to have a frank, open, satisfying self-expression, or we become repressed and cause the stream of life to flow back upon itself. The very energy which might have produced happiness and satisfaction creates stagnation and disease.

Thoughts and emotions can fester in the mind like barbs in the flesh. If this is true why should it seem strange to speak of psychic surgery and mental healing? The deep phases of the subjective life, which some psychologists call the unconscious mind, hidden almost entirely from the conscious thought, are active, creative agencies working for good or for ill.

Man is made up of the sum-total of his conscious and subconscious thoughts, plus what he inherits from his ancestors and from race thought, plus (and this is important) a spiritual inwardness. Our trouble is not derived from Life Itself, but from the use we have made of It. Life exists in Its fullness at the center of our being. If it were never blocked, It would always flow through us as life, love, harmony, happiness and success.

There is an infinite reservoir of Life within us. We may block Its passage; we may short-cut Its current, but the reservoir is still there and the flow is always ready to resume its course when we re-open the channels. Our problem is not with Life Itself, but with the use we are making of It.

The subconscious self is silently, automatically projecting our present and creating our future in accord with exact laws of cause and effect in the realm of Mind. It is working at all times on the images of thought that are given to it. But the subconscious is something that has been gradually built up. It contains only what has been put into it.

Therefore, it is possible to re-educate the subconscious. Upon what patterns of thought should this re-education be built? Surely not on the old patterns which limited us; not on the old repressions which restricted us; not on the old fears which dominated us, but, rather, on some new impulse. It is evident that these new patterns of thought must come from a source higher than the old ones. This source is what the Scripture calls "the secret place of the most High," which means a conscious and an abiding sense of our union with good.

Most of our psychic or subjective conflicts rise from a consciousness of being isolated, of being separated from our good, whether we call that good friendship, love, ideal situations, happiness, success or physical health.

The larger part of our consciousness is functioning independently of our conscious mind, as is shown in the following case history:

She was about sixty, cultured, traveled and educated. She was amply provided for financially and appeared to have good business judgment in handling her affairs. But . . . voices talked to her. It seemed as though invisible entities were tormenting her. Had I believed in spirit obsession, I should have felt that she was really obsessed. Some months before I met her, she had learned to use a ouiji board and was delighted with the messages which she received.

They were helpful and contained considerable philosophic discussion of no little merit.

Gradually she found that she could dispense with the ouiji board and communicate directly with these alleged invisible presences. But the day came when these influences, which had been so benign, became quite vicious. They began to persecute her; to tell her that because of sins she had committed, she must be punished until the sins were atoned for. It would be impossible to know just how she felt inwardly, but her experiences were real enough, so far as she was concerned. She suffered actual physical pain as a result of her inward conflict; she was not allowed to sleep at night.

Her torment had reached an excruciating stage when I first met her. I tried to tell her that these voices she heard emanated from her own subconscious self; that perhaps she had some deep-seated but unconscious sense of guilt, and that this was the way her mind was taking to condemn her. I do not think she had ever done anything very bad in her entire life, but so often we find well-meaning, honest and constructive people who entertain this deep sense of guilt. I have often felt that it might arise from the race consciousness itself; the theological condemnation of the ages; a misuse of conscience; a misconception of the beautiful relationship which the soul should have to the universe.

I found it impossible to get anywhere with this method. She insisted that she was dealing with vicious entities; that they would have to be destroyed or she would lose her reason. She feared insanity. Finding it impossible objectively to explain to her what I believed to be the seat of her trouble, I began a process of silent treatment which I felt sure would deliver her from her torment. I was thoroughly convinced then, and still am, that she was talking to herself.

I followed the line of thought that since there is but One Spirit, One Mind, which is complete and happy, and since each of us is an individual center of this God-Consciousness, there was nothing in reality that could torment her. I reasoned that there was no power, person or presence, in the flesh or out of it, which could obsess, possess or suggest anything to her, good, bad or indifferent. I took the thought that the One Mind controlled her and that the whole theory of spirit obsession or of the obsession of mental suggestion, was entirely foreign to the Truth, could not operate through her, had no power over her, no reality and no appearance of reality.

The thing did not happen in a minute. Her trouble was very deep-seated and it took some time for her to find complete emancipation, but gradually the influences waned, the voices grew less distinct. Finally, one day she met me at the door with a joyous expression on her face, exclaiming, "You know, I have had the most wonderful experience. I know that I am going to be healed. Last night the voices told me that they were not people at all; that I had been laboring under an hallucination and that you were entirely right—it has been my own subjective self that has been talking to me."

Subjective thought can fool and trap us. It can hold us in a dungeon of the self. The chief characteristic of our subjective life is its susceptibility to impression. But it is not a thing in itself; it is merely a creative medium for the action of our thought world. It can block the clear passage from the Infinite to the finite.

Psychology is making a splendid contribution in teaching us how to rebuild consciousness. But it will remain incomplete unless spiritual values are added. Man is born from something bigger than himself. If he wishes to be whole he must permit the cosmic stream to flow through him in an unobstructed channel. This is too self-evident to need elaboration. We should add to our psychological methods certain spiritual practices which consciously unite man with his infinite Source.

Fortunately for us, the subconscious reactions are something that we have built up. Therefore, we can change them. If this were not true the efforts of psychology would be futile. The psychological method alone falls short of complete fulfillment, for man must not only adjust himself to himself and to his environment, he must also make a greater adjustment, that is, to the universe itself. This calls for spiritual practice.

A meditation such as the following will be of

105

great benefit to anyone who wishes consciously to unite himself with the Source of his being:

*I am filled with the spirit of gladness.*
*I have a sense of freedom and enjoyment.*
*I am filled with an expectancy of good*
*    things.*
*The energy of Life flows through me.*
*I have no anxiety for the future, no regrets*
*    for the past.*
*For today is God's day in which I live and in*
*    which I greatly rejoice*

When one fails to express that bigger something which he feels welling up within him, he becomes, to some degree, frustrated. He becomes uneasy and unhappy. Sometimes he becomes disconsolate and morose. It naturally follows that anything which will re-establish him in a right relationship to the universe, anything which will give him an outlet for self-expression, provided it is constructive, will not only release the tension of his psychic inhibitions, it will actually release the true self.

This is why we must add spiritual practices to our psychology or we shall be dealing only with a half truth. The subconscious self is the medium between the Absolute and the relative; the automatic medium between Life and what It does for us. Fortunately, since our subconscious thought processes have all been planted, they can be uprooted and new ones put in their place.

Our subconscious self is made up of our conscious thinking, plus certain spiritual gifts with which Life has endowed us. If we think only externally we are merely loading the subconscious with more images of limitation. But if we learn to think according to certain inward patterns of thought which emanate directly from Life, we shall be neutralizing, erasing, transmuting or transforming our inward images of thought so that they may conform to the nature of the Life Principle.

It is this inner spiritual mind which the Bible refers to as the Christ, and which certain other holy books refer to as "The Illumined One." This Illumined One always dwells in the "secret place of the most High," while the external man largely dwells in the insecurity of his judgment according to appearances. Our problem, then, is to turn from the appearances and from our subjective reactions to them, which have built up images of limitation, to the center and source of our being, which is the Life Principle, God.

We may call this using the Christ Mind. We may call it spiritual illumination. It doesn't matter what we call it, so long as we remember that there is such a "secret place of the most High" within us and that we may consciously repair to it by merely knowing that we are already there. This is the place where the universe meets us in its wholeness without any restriction whatsoever. This is the place where the All delivers everything that It is to us.

Anything which helps you to do this is good. If you say prayers, make affirmations, repeat beautiful passages, or merely sit in the quiet contemplation of your thought, realizing the presence of Life, you will do well, for all of these methods lead to the conclusion that the Power exists and is available.

All life, all health, all peace and all possibility, exist in this Power. It is a knowledge of this and the conscious use of this knowledge which will give freedom. Our loneliness, our sense of isolation, our poverty, doubt and sickness, are results of being disconnected from the fullness of this Divine Self.

Never think that you can live disconnected from that which is Life. If you wish to call this conscious union with Life *religion*, well and good, for it is the essence of every religion. If you wish to call conscious union with the wholeness of things *spirituality*, well and good, for it is the very essence of spirituality. But don't be afraid of the terms. We need not create a new religion to do this. We do not have to deny any physical fact. We wish to become whole and we cannot become whole while our consciousness isolates us from the Principle of Wholeness.

God is not only an infinite Presence, the Spirit is also an indwelling reality. The silent whisperings of this inner Presence come to each as a divine revelation, an inner communion of the individual spirit with the *Over-Soul;* that vast and invisible Presence in which we live, move and have our being.

The Upanishads inform us that "by the knowledge of God the bonds of ignorance and unhappiness are destroyed." The Talmud says, "Pray not that sinners may perish, but that the sin itself may disappear." This means that evil has no existence in itself, for if we persist in seeing the true rather than the false, then the false will disappear and the true will make its appearance. In the midst of confusion there is a place of peace. In the midst of sorrow the joy of life persists.

The Science of Mind teaches us to look for good instead of evil; to praise and not to condemn; to bless and curse not; to live each day as though the Spirit were guiding us; to have a firm conviction that we are counseled by Divine Wisdom and protected by Infinite Love. We should at all times sense this overshadowing Presence and have implicit confidence in Its direction.

No matter what the doubts and fears of yesterday were, the affirmations of today may rise triumphant over them. If we persist in seeing beauty, beauty will appear. Let us no longer weep over the mistakes of yesterday. This is futile. We must learn to forgive ourselves even as we forgive others. Let us remember that "each day is a fresh beginning, every day is the world made new." It makes no difference how unhappy or fearful we may have been in the past, today presents itself with a new opportunity; today we may start life afresh. Thus hope overcomes despair, faith vanquishes fear and defeat is swallowed up in victory.

Just as, when we are tired physically, a bath in fresh running water invigorates us, so, when we are tired or discomforted mentally, spiritual communion, bathing in the ocean of the Infinite, invigorates the mind and clarifies the thinking. Every person should take time for this inner communion, time when he separates himself from all that appears evil or negative, time to plunge into the living waters of his Being. Just as we take a sun bath, so there is an inner light into which we may plunge, an inner consciousness in which we may bathe. The rays of this invisible Sun penetrate the soul just as the rays of the physical sun penetrate the body, renewing and rejuvenating. As water purifies itself by flowing, so an inner realization of the flow of Spirit through us purifies the stagnant pools of morbid thought, and in so doing, eliminates stagnation in the physical body.

As travelers crossing the desert, covered with dust and filled with weariness, seek the refreshment of an oasis, the shelter of a rock in a weary land, the cool shade under a spreading palm, so the mind, weary with confusion, exhausted with too much effort, must seek a spiritual oasis, an inner communion with the Invisible. This oasis is at the center of every man's life. There is the shelter of a rock in every man's soul. No one yet has ever turned to this place without finding comfort.

Let us dare to plunge into this invisible stream of Life, to bathe in its waters. Let us resolve to put aside the cares and worries that have fretted us. Let us seek the solace, the comfort and the peace of communion with the *Over-Soul*—the conscious union of our mind with the mind of the Universe.

Do not wonder whether you are becoming religious or spiritual. These things should not be self-conscious anyway. Just wonder if you are getting right with yourself and with the universe. If getting right with yourself and with the universe is religion, then it is at least a good religion, since it judges no one, condemns no one and fears nothing. If living in harmony and unity with Life is spirituality, then no doubt that is what we need. But remember, the Power is delivered only on Its own terms. We cannot make It something which It is not; we can only accept It as It is.

There is something deeper than the intellect, something which cannot and need not be rationalized; it is something which must be accepted. True salvation lies not in any outward form but in some inward grace whereby we become consciously one with the All Good. In this sense, then, we shall have to become as a little child. We shall have to be conscious of our union with good. We shall have to feel our oneness with the Power.

The vital secret in every religion lies in the recognition that the Spirit of Life is ever present—where the need is, there also is its answer—where the prob-

111

lem is, there also is its solution. "Whither shall I go from Thy presence, or whither shall I flee from Thy spirit?"

Perhaps our great mistake has been that we have tried to locate this secret place outside the self. If so, we must turn our spiritual gaze inward. Peace, poise and consciousness of power in right action come only through a consciousness of partnership with the Eternal. The secret place of the most High is not a location, but a state of thought, an interior awareness, a spiritual faith.

Man is a center in the Consciousness of God, and since God is everywhere it naturally follows that we always stand at the threshold of divine Wisdom, infinite Peace and perfect Power. We may enter in and possess this kingdom of good if we have the will to do so. But first we must have faith that such a kingdom exists. Here is where the soul, as Emerson said, makes its great claim on God. We must dare to believe not only that there is a secret place of the most High, but that we are in it now.

Is it, then, so difficult to believe in good instead of evil; to have faith in victory rather than fear of defeat? What if our problems are great, individually and collectively, is there not One greater than all these difficulties? Truly the "secret place of the most High" is wherever our faith rivets its attention with assurance; wherever our conviction sees through that which denies the reign of right. Let us open up an ever-widening channel for this Divine Influx, and remaining calm in the midst of the storm, let us go forward to the greater good.

In actual practice suppose you find yourself confronted by a problem which you seem unable to solve.

> *Instead of thinking about the problem, turn from it to a recognition that the Life Principle has no problems.*
> *Know that the Mind within you already understands the solution to this problem.*
> *State definitely that the Mind within you knows what to do.*
> *Affirm that you are inwardly guided by the supreme Intelligence of the universe.*
> *Affirm that everything you ought to know you do know.*
> *Affirm that you are compelled to make right decisions.*
> *Know that there is something within you which will not permit you to make a mistake.*

I once met a man who was competing for the working out of certain chemical formulas necessary to the industry in which he was interested. He had been working without avail over a period of several months and had come to a dead end.

I asked him to stop any conscious effort for a few days and to go up on top of the apartment house where he lived each night and look up at the stars. I asked him to think how big everything is; how wonderful the Intelligence must be which conceives and governs this vast cosmic activity. I asked him not to think about his problem as though it were difficult, but to turn within himself and say: "The Intelligence which creates and sustains all this is now acquainting my mind with the perfect answer to this particular problem."

I also worked for him (treated him mentally), affirming that Divine Intelligence is now working through his thought; is now directing his every movement. I affirmed that his problem was not a problem but was merely an opportunity for a greater self-expression. In less than a week he had the answer. It was complete.

This illustration shows us how necessary it is not to attach our problems to the Divine Mind, but to unite the Divine Mind with the answer to the problem, for there is a vast difference. Principles have no problems. Therefore, in a sense, we subject our finite problems to the Infinite Intelligence which automatically solves them through our recognition and acceptance that they are being solved.

In actual practice this means that we rearrange our thinking in such a way that we permit new ideas to flow in. The ideas, fears and tensions that obstructed this flow are released. The stream flows free again. It is in this sense that God is the answer to every human problem.

Emerson tells us that we must beware lest we hold too much good in our hands. We must scatter it, he says, on every wind of heaven. Whitman said, "The gift is most to the giver and comes back most to him." Jesus proclaimed, "Give, and it shall be given unto you." It is the nature of Life that the more widely we use It, the more of It is delivered into our keeping for use.

Every time we use the Law of Life in a constructive manner, we widen our channels for self-expression—they become broader and deeper. Denying the Law of Life temporarily blocks Its flow through us. Spiritual faith opens up the use of this Law as no other mental attitude can. Therefore, the thing to do is to live in conscious and enthusiastic recognition of Life, to live in faith.

# Chapter X

DID YOU ever read a little article called *The Scent of Fear?* In it the author says that animals will attack us only when we are afraid of them. Fear exudes a subtle scent which the animal smells. This arouses a corresponding fear in him and he makes the attack for self-protection. I have known persons who could walk through swarms of bees and never be stung because they had no fear. I have a friend who has no fear of snakes; he sat on a rock, under which a rattlesnake was coiled, while he drew some plans.

The person who fears life gets but little pleasure from living. The antidote for fear is faith. The man with great faith has no fear. Faith is a mental attitude, hence it can be cultivated.

There are certain fundamental fears from which most of us suffer. We are afraid of pain. We are afraid of poverty. We are afraid of being misunderstood, and perhaps we fear that we are not immortal. All fear finally rests upon some uncertainty about the welfare of the self. Will people understand and love us? Shall we find friendship? Shall we be successful? Shall we be happy? Shall we be prosperous? And, when in the due course of time, we "shuffle off this mortal coil," will it be but a transition from one state to another, or shall we pass into oblivion? Anyone who can answer these questions to his own satisfaction will have overcome the major fears of life.

Let us consider the fear of being misunderstood. This is a problem which affects many people. If we wish only good toward others, why should we expect them to wish anything other than good toward us? Generally speaking, the world meets us as we meet it, reflecting back to us our own mental attitudes toward it. Let us expect people to be friendly and refuse to have our feelings hurt.

The best way to make friends is to realize that we meet Life in everyone. The God in us meets the God in others. Proclaiming the Divine Presence, believing in It, we shall meet It. Love will find a perfect way. Our faith in the Divine Presence in others will overcome the fear of being misunderstood, and we shall no longer have our feelings hurt.

If the mind is calm and serene there will be less liability toward pain. Therefore, at all times we should be serene and poised. But suppose we go a little deeper than this and realize that there must be a Divine Pattern of Life at the center of every organ, of every cell in the human body. The flow of blood represents the flow of Life; the nervous system represents the flow of Divine Intelligence. The body is an instrument of the Spirit, an avenue for Its self-expression. The body is a temple of God. With this realization fear and pain will disappear; physical functions of the body will react accordingly and most of our diseases will disappear.

Confidence and love alone cast out fear. The man without fear is the only truly whole man. It is ours to decide whether we shall live in fear or in faith. Let us decide to live in faith. Let the keynote of our thought be, "The Lord is my light and my salvation; whom shall I fear? the Lord is the strength of my life; of whom shall I be afraid?" Faith alone can bind us back to the Invisible. Let us learn to practice faith until all fear disappears, until life ceases to be a funeral dirge and becomes a song of joy.

We feel cut off from the Source of our being when we fail daily to reunite ourselves with the Source of all being. This is the meaning of true religion, disregarding its outward form, for the body of Truth is one, no matter what vestments it may wear.

To find peace in the midst of confusion, one must realize his center in pure Spirit. To reach this place of confidence and faith in the midst of doubt and uncertainty, one must establish himself in the conviction that the Divine keeps watch over Its own. The center of every man's life is poised in pure Spirit. We should daily seek this inner communion for it is also a place of spiritual protection and divine guidance.

We are immersed in a creative and living Intelligence, the Intelligence that creates and sustains the vast cosmic order, holding the planets in their appointed orbits, governing the wind and the wave. This Intelligence is ours to use. We may use the Power of the Divine Mind by consciously thinking It into manifestation. We should realize that the unerring judgment of Divine Intelligence directs our lives, making perfect and plain the way before us.

The energy of spiritual power must be hooked up to conscious intention if our faith in it is going to become justified by actual objective results. Suppose you say today:

> *I know that God is within me.*
> *I know that the Spirit within me is perfect.*
> *I enter into Its peace and am secure in Its protection.*
> *The unerring judgment of Divine Intelligence directs my way.*

We should consciously unite our thought with the Divine Mind and consciously unite the creative Law of the Divine Mind with our affairs. If we can do this we are certain to succeed. Any statement you use which helps you to do this will be effective.

When the Bible says, "Let this mind be in you, which was also in Christ Jesus," it is referring to that Spirit within us which is our personal share of the universal Spirit. The Christ Mind does not refer merely to a personality who lived two thousand years ago. It also refers to the innermost principle of our own being. It refers to the Divine Presence centered in us. We have been told to put off the old man and put on the new man, which is Christ. This new man is our innermost self. Pure Spirit exists at the very center of our being, at the innermost part of our mind. It is our true and eternal Self. Such life as we have flows from It. There is nothing to our real being other than Life and what It does through us.

The secret about the use of Its Power is no secret at all. It is merely that we recognize Its presence and consciously use It; consciously speak this Power into manifestation through our word. This is what is meant by making a demonstration, or, if you choose to state it this way, by the answer to prayer. To make a demonstration means to bring some good into our experience which, up until now, we have not been experiencing other than in a limited manner, or which we have not had at all; to make some dream, some secret desire of the heart, come true.

What do you suppose would happen to the world if everyone came to realize that pure Spirit is at the center of his being? This we cannot say, but individually we may experiment with ourselves and discover what will happen in our individual experience, through the realization of the Divine Presence active in our thought.

Isaiah said, if you do this, "Thy sun shall no more

go down . . . for the Lord shall be thine everlasting light, and the days of thy mourning shall be ended." St. Gregory tells us that the *sun* signifies the illumination of truth. The *sun* stands for the inner spiritual Principle. When this sun shines, all obstructions are removed. This poetic utterance of Isaiah represents the everlasting sun of truth as the incarnation of God within each one of us, which the Bible calls *The Christ*.

The sun is always shining and when we withdraw ourselves from the shadows of our unbelief, we shall find that the "days of our mourning" will be ended. Mourning suggests that something has been lost. We are sad because we have lost a loved one; we have lost our health, our fortune or something else that we hold dear. Isaiah suggests that our days of mourning will cease when we view the universe as it really is.

"Wilt thou be made whole?" asked the great teacher. Standing in the midst of the multitude, he proclaimed that the kingdom of God is at hand. Perhaps there is not so great a gulf between heaven and earth as we have believed. Are we taking time daily to permit the sunshine of truth to penetrate the dark chambers of our mind? "Wilt thou be made whole?" is a suggestion to open the windows of our mind, to lift up the gates of our consciousness, that the eternal flow of light may find entrance.

Buddha said, "This light is like a medicine in destroying the poison of human corruption. It is like water in removing dirt and defilement. It is like a magic jewel in giving all good fortune." Jesus referred to it as "the pearl of great price." This light is not something we go in search of; it is already within the self. This is why the Bible refers to man as "a candle of the Lord."

Spiritual man is perfect. There is a Divine Pattern hidden at the center of our being. "Be ye therefore perfect, even as your Father which art in heaven is perfect." The wick of our being runs deep into the oil of Spirit.

Through pure intuition you know that there is a "secret place of the most High" within you; that you can move up into this place and abide there in perfect safety. This does not mean that you are to withdraw from outward acts, for only those who are maladjusted to life retire from living.

It is a natural desire to enter more fully into life; to enter into a state of greater livingness, a more complete self-expression. The very desire you have to do this rises from the urge of the Life which is incarnated in you.

Life at the center of your being is a silent Power. It comes to you as feeling, as conviction, as an inward awareness. Whenever you speak from this inward awareness, consciously recognizing that all the Power that there is, is flowing through your words, then you endow your words with great power.

You should take time daily to rise above any

sense of confusion. As you do this, you will feel a stillness at the center of your being. As you sense this inner stillness you will feel the Power moving out into action, in everything you think. Have absolute faith that It will do this and you will not be disappointed.

You are not entering into this silent place for the purpose of asking the Law of Life to be power. It already is power. You are recognizing this Power and permitting It to flow into action through your word.

Just what is meant by "your word"? It means your conscious intention, your conscious direction, your conscious faith and acceptance that, because of what you are doing, the Power will flow through your word in the direction you give It.

In the Science of Mind we call this giving a treatment. This does not mean that we are holding thoughts. It does not mean that we are concentrating the Power. It does not mean that we are willing something to happen. It does mean that we are providing a condition in our consciousness (our thought world) which permits the Power to flow through us. It will always flow through us when we provide the right condition.

You are not beseeching It, you are thinking It into manifestation. Perhaps, when you sit in the silence of your thought, many ideas will come racing through your mind, many confusing concepts; ideas of limitation and fear and a sense of uncertainty may rise in consciousness. Brush these ideas aside mentally—not as though you were fighting them, but more as though you were seeing through them.

Physical facts, forms and conditions are no obstruction to this Principle. It flows through them and takes a new form in them. It remolds them. That which makes can re-make; that which molds can remold; that which creates can re-create. Remember, what you see comes from what you do not see. The visible is the Invisible made manifest. It is the Invisible caught in temporary form. Every time you think you are giving form to this Invisible Power.

Lay aside all sense of unworthiness. Do not say, "I wonder if I am good enough to use this Power." You are using It anyway. Since It is you, you cannot stop using It. It is not only the Mind *into* which you think, It is the Mind *by* which you think. This is why your thought is creative.

Any thought, word or statement, any affirmation or denial, any inspirational idea which helps you to rise above the confusion of outward circumstances, is good. Many persons have risen·above confusion by repeating the Lord's Prayer or the Twenty-third Psalm, or by saying, "The Power (God) is all there is." However, there is no magic in any of these statements. The magic, which seems to be in them, is not in the statements themselves but in the state of thought they induce. In so far as you have belief, faith and acceptance, you can turn to an obstacle and by declaring that it is not a thing in itself, and by affirming its exact opposite with complete conviction, you may see the obstruction dissolve and a new form take its place.

When one works with himself consistently and persistently, using statements which convey the proper meaning to his own mind, something happens. If not quickly, then gradually, an inner subjective embodiment of the idea stated takes form, and this inner subjective embodiment sets the creative Law in motion for the definite purpose specified.

Let your consciousness rise above the sense of separation from the Power, and in a few moments you will feel as though you were sitting in the midst of an infinite sea of unobstructed Life. This place in Mind where you now are is the Source of all action, is the center of all creativity. It is also the innermost part of your own being.

Above everything else realize you are doing a spontaneously natural thing. Just as a plant turns to the sun, your thoughts turn to the Power and draw It down through your being, causing It to manifest through your word. In this act you are not losing your identity, you are more intensely self-conscious than ever before, but you are conscious in a larger, less obstructed manner. Whatever you decree, state or affirm, from this altitude of thought, will produce definite results.

The Law of Life exists in all of us at all times and we are using It whether or not we are conscious of the fact. If we wish to make specific demonstrations we must use It specifically. That is, if one wishes to demonstrate a home he should work definitely to know that he has such a home. This should not merely be an abstract statement such as saying, "Heaven is my home." He wishes a temporary home here on earth, therefore, in his treatment, which means the mental statements he makes to himself, he should definitely specify that the Divine Mind is creating a home for him.

In such statements he should specify that:

*This home is a place of beauty.*
*It is a place where love reigns supreme.*
*It is a place of co-operation, mutual admiration and helpfulness.*
*It is a home of love and peace.*
*It is a home of confidence and trust.*
*It is a home of joy and happiness.*

A specific mental treatment for definite purposes means, stating in your own words, and believing in your mind that exactly what you wish to happen is going to happen. A treatment is a definite thing. The mind is affirming a desired condition as though it already existed. Jesus said that when we pray we should actually believe that we already possess the object of our desire. Nothing could be plainer, more simple or direct than this.

Affirmation should always refer to the present time and not to some state of futurity. Each treatment should conclude with as complete a realization of the Divine Presence as possible. There should be a sense of calm, of peace and of joy accompanying every treatment. There should be a deep realization of the Divine Presence, but the treatment itself should be specific.

In giving a treatment—

*Try to relax mentally and physically.*

*When you do this, you will find something very definite taking place in your thought world.*

*Solid facts become fluid; obstructions and obstacles seem to fall away.*

*You are, in a sense, climbing a ladder of thought which perhaps started in dense confusion, fear and uncertainty.*

*The first step takes you a little above this confusion, and now you begin to climb more easily.*

*There is an enthusiastic elasticity in your step.*

*You climb joyously.*

*You find that you have passed through the clouds of fear, despair and doubt.*

*There is light everywhere.*

Try to sense that there is no difference between your thought, the flow of the Power through your thought, and the manifestation of the Power in your experience, or in the experience of the one you wish to help. For instance, if you say, "Right action exists there," wherever you designate, try to have complete confidence that right action does exist there. If something within you denies this right action, declare that there is no truth in this denial, and immediately affirm right action.

Because the Power is in your word, your word has the authority to dissipate or dissolve any wrong action. If you are doing this for yourself merely state, "This is for myself," or "This is the truth about me." If your desire is to help someone else merely state, "This is for him (or for her)." Make your statements calmly, deliberately, distinctly, and hold them in your consciousness until they seem real to you. This is what is meant by abiding in faith.

There is a place in everyone where this Power abides in Its fullness. You are merely distributing it. We have a parallel law for this in physics. We catch the power from the waterfall, we do not create it. We call this generating it. We transform it then, do we not, into a mechanical energy, and then we distribute it. We direct it for light and heat and motive power. In one place it runs a street car, in another it heats an electric flatiron. The power already existed, we are merely using it.

This law in physics has a parallel in your own mind. Your belief and acceptance generate a Power which already exists. Your conscious recognition of this Power causes It to flow through your thought, while your conscious intention directs It into whatever channel you choose and for whatever purpose you decide.

Always you are using the Power and always It is flowing through you without effort, either to Itself or to you. This is the meaning of the saying, "Be still and know that I am God (the Power)." If in doing this you become confused with other thoughts, just quietly push them aside. Don't fight them, don't be antagonized by them, don't resist them. Just let them pass by like floating clouds. Keep pouring the penetrating rays of your thought upon them until they dissipate.

Your thought is clear only when you are thinking from the standpoint of the unobstructed Power. Your mind is using the X-ray of a Power which knows no obstruction.

When an engineer converts the energy of coal, wood, oil, wind or wave, he is not using will power. He is using conscious decision coupled with the definite knowledge of the energy with which he is dealing.

*Instead of will he has a willingness.*
*Instead of holding the power he is loosing it.*
*Instead of concentrating it he is merely gathering it up and loosing it again.*

So it is in the realm of thoughts and ideas, for they are the mechanical instruments of the mind,

129

which generate and distribute a Power that already exists.

The statements you make are not made for the purpose of convincing the Power. They are made for the purpose of distributing It. The only thing you have to convince is your own thought. The only thing you have to convert is your own unbelief. The only obstruction you will meet is in your own imagination. There is nothing in the universe that can keep you from using this Power but yourself.

# Chapter XI

YOUR PLACE in Life is to become an outlet for Its wisdom, intelligence, love, beauty and creativeness.

Your relationship to Life is that you are of like nature to It. You are in It and It is in you. Some part of you exists as pure, unmanifest Spirit. This side of your nature is superior to anything that happens to you. You can prove this easily enough by this simple experiment. Some day when you feel depressed, unhappy, or melancholy, sit quietly by yourself and begin mentally to climb up out of your difficulties. Push your thought up through every obstruction, practicing the affirmations and denials which have been used in this book, and your sense of depression and fear will fade away.

If you continue in this practice long enough, you will find yourself emerging in some part of your being which has never been troubled. You will be demonstrating that some part of you lives above confusion. Through this simple act you will have demonstrated that you have the freedom to be unhappy, and that you also have the freedom to convert this unhappiness into joy. You will be proving that you are an individual, but an individual who can draw on an invisible Power.

Power that is unused remains dormant; it is merely a possibility. But we are using the Power of Life at all times whether or not we are aware of the fact. Here is the case of a woman who was using It wrongly.

I have never seen a funnier spectacle than she presented, stretched out on the bed with a hot water bottle poised on her stomach. I couldn't help it, I sat down and burst out laughing. If she hadn't had a sense of humor she never would have liked me. But that was many years ago and she has been one of my best friends ever since.

We were living in a small cottage at the beach and one day when I was in Pasadena (twenty miles from where we lived) lecturing, my mother phoned me and said that a Mrs. . . . . had arrived bag and baggage, with the declaration that she had come to be healed. Naturally, my mother told her that we were not running a private sanitarium and it was impossible for us to receive guests since we only had a small cottage. But all to no avail. I have always admired her persistence. She just wouldn't take "no" for an answer, therefore she didn't have to. She came and she stayed.

When I returned, just before dinner, my mother said, "She is upstairs."

It all seemed quite ridiculous and absurd, but up I went and there she was, spread out on the bed. She was fully dressed. Great tears were streaming down her face. She was a large woman and that hot water bottle perched on her stomach was one of the funniest things I have ever seen. I should have had to laugh if she had died that very moment. Perhaps this is one of nature's ways of relieving a tense situation. Tears and laughter—what relief they often bring. Naturally, she was surprised at my laughter.

"What in the world are you laughing at?" she asked.

"You," I replied, "I am laughing at you. I can't help it."

She really had a great sense of humor—a God-given gift. She burst out laughing, too, even in the midst of her pain and tears.

The history of her case: Several years before this incident, it had been necessary for her to have an abdominal operation. It was believed at that time that she could not possibly survive. She came out of the anesthetic into a moment's consciousness just long enough to hear one of the nurses remark that in all probability she would pass on between four and five o'clock in the afternoon. She again lapsed into an unconscious state. However, she lived and apparently got well. She had been operated upon by one of the finest surgeons in America and he was in no way responsible for what followed. It was just one of those things that happen, but it does have great significance in showing us how the laws of mind work.

She recovered from her operation but about three months after that, every afternoon between four and five she would be seized with severe abdominal pains, excruciating agony, tremendous gas pressure and a physical discomfort which racked her whole being. Possibly it was all in her imagination, but it certainly appeared to be in her body. What difference does it make where the pain is, if it hurts? You will never heal anyone by merely telling him that his trouble is just in his mind or imagination, for whatever the seat of the trouble is, it must be dealt with intelligently.

Fortunately, in this case, within an hour we had a complete analysis and apparently a correct one, since she was healed that very night. Within two weeks she was perfectly normal and the physical symptoms from which she had suffered have never returned.

I explained to her that when she regained consciousness in the hospital long enough to hear one of the nurses say she would probably pass on between four and five that afternoon, that remark registered in her subconscious—that part of her which never went to sleep, that part of her which acted as though everything she heard were true and which tried to make everything which she believed come true in her experience. We might say that her pain was psychic, and so it was in its origin, but it produced its physical correspondent with mathematical precision and exacted an awful toll from her physical and mental endurance.

In this instance, very little silent treatment was necessary. The explanation seemed to be sufficient to meet the case, to uncover the cause, and to enable her to regain her psychic equilibrium. I often wonder how many of our internal disorders are of similar nature.

As you look into the vast physical universe you will observe that definite manifestations of life take place in certain locations in space. It is self-evident that Life localizes Itself in form through some action within Itself. This action has been called the Word of God.

Since you are fashioned from the stuff of the Invisible, Its nature is incarnated in you. Because of this, your word has the power, in your world, of localizing itself, of manifesting itself in concrete form.

*You are in Life.*
*Life is flowing through you.*
*It is you.*
*It decrees, speaks, announces, affirms, thinks, knows, images (all of which have an identical meaning).*
*That which It decrees transpires.*

135

*You are like It.*
*You rule your own world.*

If there is any confusion in your mind about this, just ask yourself, "Where does anything come from?" Science, as well as revelation, announces that there is a vast cosmic energy equally distributed throughout space. Some movement takes place within this energy, some vibration which science, as well as revelation, announces can be thought of only in the terms of infinite Mind or Intelligence operating upon Itself. This is not difficult to understand. It is the very essence of simplicity. It is an unavoidable conclusion.

Realizing that all creation is a result of this original Life and that creation is now going on—plants are growing in the garden, planets are being formed, hair is growing on your head, creation is something that is always taking place—and that you are some part of this creative order, what is more reasonable to assume than that the movement of your thought upon your environment projects that environment. This is the substance of this whole teaching.

You wish goodness instead of evil, health instead of disease, success instead of limitation, joy in the place of sorrow. Life is all these things, and being all these things, and having an intense desire within Itself to be expressed, It presses against you desiring your freedom, your joy and your wholeness. It would be untrue to Its nature for It to desire anything less than this. Life is for you, Its power is on your side. You have as much power to use as you believe in.

Since Life, acting as Law, has no personal intention for you other than the one you give It, it logically follows that there must be a definite idea in your mind, a definite belief or acceptance. This is why we have been told that in effective prayer we must believe even though we do not yet possess. This will not be difficult to do if we get it firmly fixed in our thought that the Law of Mind operates upon our belief and projects a form corresponding to this belief.

Every idea automatically sets the Law of Life in motion in such a way as to produce this and not some other idea. There is something involved in a sunflower seed which acts upon the creative energy of nature in such a way as to produce a sunflower and not a cabbage or a potato. Definite ideas produce definite results.

This means that if you are using this Law to bring friendship into someone's life, then you are specializing It for this definite purpose and not for something or someone else. Because you are definitely affirming that as a result of your word love and friendship will be brought into his experience, then the Law will bring to him the love and friendship implied in your thought.

Let us illustrate this in another way. Someone asks you to plant corn in his garden. You go over to his plot of ground and plant corn there. You are definitely specializing a creative law which will produce corn in *his* garden, not in some *other* person's garden. Your whole intention has been to take seed corn, go over to his plot of ground and plant it for him. You know that corn will now grow in *his* garden. This corn is going to grow in his garden and not in some other person's garden. It is going to grow there because you have planted it there for him. Of course he could refuse to permit you to plant his garden. He could pull up the young stocks of corn and destroy the possibility of a harvest. Nothing else, however, could hinder the operation of the Law for him.

The following is a suggested procedure for helping another:

1. Relax mentally and physically. Free your mind of any sense of strain and hurry. Recognize that there is one supreme Source of power which is Spirit, Life and Infinite Intelligence.
2. Know that your word is the presence, the power and the activity of the supreme Law of Life now operating through the one you wish to help.
3. Recognize that he is one with, and a definite part of, this perfect Life, this supreme Intelligence, and this infinite Harmony. Make this recognition as complete as possible, using any thoughts that will help you. It is not the particular words you use but the consciousness of the meaning of these words which gives power to your treatment.
4. Recognize that the truth about this person is al-

ready established in pure Spirit. You are going to recognize that which already is the truth about his real nature.

5. Declare that your word is the Law of Spirit establishing harmony and right adjustment in his life. NOTE: Conform your statements to meet his need. Your statement is the law of adjustment to all personal, family, business or professional affairs in his life. Declare that the Source of all life is manifesting in and through him.

6. If treating for success or the control of conditions, affirm that success and prosperity are the Law of his being. He is governed by pure Intelligence and inspired by divine Wisdom. He is guided into right action and compelled to make right decisions. He is surrounded by friendship, love and beauty. There is a continuous sense of enthusiastic joy, of abundant vitality and of inspiration in everything he does.

7. If treating for physical conditions, conform your statements to meet the needs of the one you are helping. Realize that every organ, action and function of his physical being represent the divine Life manifesting through him. Develop the thought that just as there is but One Mind which governs everything intelligently, this Mind is the Mind of God, so there is but One Body through which this Mind functions. The body of your patient is the Body of God. It is perfect, indestructible and divine. Develop the idea that

limitless enthusiasm, vitality and life are forever flowing through him. Realize that there is perfect circulation, perfect assimilation and perfect elimination. Do not hesitate to deny the reality of any wrong action, being careful, however, that in place of the wrong action you supply an idea of right action.

8. Reaching the conclusion of your treatment, realize that what you have done is real, is true, is established, is perfect, changeless and permanent. Following this there should be a complete but active state of mental silence in which you realize the Truth which you have spoken.

You will become increasingly conscious of this Power by the increasing use you make of It. You will grow in faith through demonstration. The secret of the whole thing is to believe that you can. Remember limitation never came out of the Law of Life. Limitation came from a certain use of a Power which, Itself, is limitless. The Law has never changed; you are merely changing your position in It.

The Law will always serve us. It has no intention or purpose contrary to our best good, but the Law of Life is a real law and we cannot go contrary to Its principle and hope to get an affirmative result. We cannot deny our affirmations without temporarily destroying their effects.

It is our business to convert failure into success; to transmute disease into life-giving wholeness; to neutralize the effects of fear and sorrow through an inner awareness of joy and peace. We are taking everything that does not belong to the great Reality and trading it in, as it were, for that which ought to be. We are swapping old ideas for new ones.

This is what is meant by "dying daily," for every day and every hour some part of our thought world passes out of existence, some new portion is born. It matters not what the harvest of last year was, today is a new seed time, tomorrow holds the promise of a new harvest.

# Chapter XII

You DO not have to struggle. You have discovered that Life works through a Law of Mind, and how your thought automatically is acted upon by this Law. You can now transfer the burden of personal responsibility into the Law.

You have a partnership with the Invisible. Your silent partner, the Law of Mind, will always create the good you desire for yourself or others, when you comply with Its nature.

It is right that you live a more abundant life. The more largely you live the more completely Life Itself will be expressed through you. It is right that we all should seek greater happiness for ourselves and for others.

We may, then, unhesitatingly transfer the sense of personal burden, placing it upon the shoulders of the Law which is able, always ready and ever willing to work for us. This is not selfishness but self-expression. Man exists that Life through him may more completely express Itself. Therefore, in expressing ourselves we are expressing It.

Be careful to differentiate between the Law of Mind and the Spirit. The Law of Mind is a mathematical and impersonal force operating upon your thought images. This Law is like other laws of nature and should be thought of in this light. Life Itself is a spiritual Presence in the universe—the Infinite Person back of all personality. It is warm, colorful and responsive. It is the essence of love, beauty and wisdom. If we live close to Its nature we shall always be using the Law of Mind constructively and only good can follow.

The goodness of Life does not deny the operation of the law of cause and effect. The goodness of God does not deny the operation of natural laws. Throughout the ages, unfortunately, there has been great confusion because people have not realized that the karmic law of cause and effect is different from the Spirit—just as electric energy is different from the electrician, just as an engine is different from the engineer.

The nature of Life is such that the universe is filled with an infinite Presence and permeated with a limitless Law. From this Presence, which is pure Spirit, we receive counsel, guidance and comfort. The Law of Mind, like any other law in nature, is our servant and we should use It with complete authority. Whenever we use It destructively we shall automatically be punished. Not that Life punishes us, but that we punish ourselves through the ignorant use of the Law of Mind.

We should think of the Divine Presence as infinite joy, beauty and wisdom. We should think of the Law as a limitless capacity to create for us. Always desiring good for ourselves and others, we should have no hesitation in imposing our desires upon the Law, that they may become fulfilled.

The only limit the Law has in working for us, is that It must work through us. Life can only give us what we take. The taking is a thing of faith and understanding. We may be certain then:

> If our thoughts are always constructive we shall always be divinely guided.
> If our thoughts are always affirmative the Law will always respond affirmatively.
> If we live in inward peace we shall never be confused.
> If faith dominates our consciousness we shall never be afraid.
> If we are always kind we shall never know hate.
> If we think of life as an eternal springtime, forever blossoming anew into self-expression through us, we shall never grow old.

The greatest good that can come to anyone is to realize his true relationship with the Spirit of Life and

with the Law which is Its servant. Spirit is Life Itself, the Law is the way It works.

I trust you will forgive this repetition, but it
seems so necessary to me that we differentiate between the Thing Itself, the Infinite Person, and our
use of the Law which is an infinite, but impersonal
and creative force in nature. We already do this in
dealing with other natural laws. We should learn to
think of spiritual and mental laws in the terms of
natural laws.

The farmer does this when he sows his crop. Experience has taught him that he can sow this crop
with certainty of a harvest. In this way he transfers
the burden of creation into the law by placing his
desire there as an already fulfilled fact. He has complete faith in this law. Experience has taught him
that if he wishes to harvest corn, corn is what he
must plant.

In dealing with the Law of Mind, experience has
taught us that when we furnish the Law with an idea,
It creates the form of that idea. The burden of crea-
tion is not upon our shoulders; it is within the great
Law of cause and effect. We must have faith in this
Law. We must abandon ourselves to It.

In Bunyan's *Pilgrim's Progress*, you will remember that the pilgrim started his journey at the foot of
a mountain with a heavy load on his shoulders. As
he gradually made the ascent this load fell from him,
and finally disappeared entirely as he reached the
summit. So we shall find that whatever our burdens

may have been while in the valley of despair, or in the canyon of bewilderment, they will fall from us as we reach the summit of spiritual realization.

This ascent, which Bunyan so beautifully characterized, has a meaning identical with that in the Scriptures where we are told to go up into the mount. It was this mountain into which Moses went when he received the inspiration to write the great code of law. It was this mountain into which Jesus went to gain his final triumph over everything which denied the goodness and power of Life. Your mountain is the innermost sanctuary of your thought world.

In actual practice this is what you should do:

> Begin mentally to climb into a spiritual atmosphere, dropping all burdens, anxieties, fears and doubts behind you.
> You will soon discover that, as your thought reaches a place of peace, confusion disappears.
> From this inner place of peace you speak your word, which is to become the law unto that whereunto it is spoken.

The highest consciousness is not one of possession, but of being. The greater your consciousness of being, the more automatically will the Law flow from this consciousness into the acquisition of the things you desire.

The highest use of Life is not an act of will, of

concentration, nor of holding thoughts. These attitudes suggest burdens. They suggest the coercion of a reluctant power. They suggest the necessity of putting power into your word. These attitudes are directly opposite to those you should assume. You are not putting power into your word, you are taking power out of it, just as the generator takes power out of the waterfall. The power is already there.

The more completely you realize the presence of this Power, the more of It you will generate. Hence, the more of It you will have to distribute. The power which flows from your word is in mathematical proportion to your recognition of the Power flowing into your word. This is why we must have faith. This is why all things are possible if we do have faith.

The Law of Itself does nothing without a word, a thought, or an idea. It has no impulsion of Its own. Just as the empty lot next to your house produces nothing of itself but is ever ready to produce when it is planted, so the Law of your mind waits until It becomes impregnated with the creative word which sets it in motion. Your word differentiates this Law. The Law of Life is not Life Itself, just as the engine is not the engineer.

Now that we have come to understand the operation of the Law of Life; now that we realize every word we speak has some power, we should ever be seeking the word that has all power. If we wish to discover that word we must first lose sight of ourselves as isolated, separated beings. It is not from the thought of the little you and the little me, separated from Life, that the greatest use of the Law comes, but from an expansion of consciousness through which we contemplate Life as one vast wholeness. We are one with the Spirit of Life, one with Its Law and one with Its manifestation.

Our word of power can be spoken in fullness only as we recognize the unity of all life, only as the good we desire for the self includes all others. This does not mean that we should hesitate to use the Law for personal benefits, for the Law responds to everyone who uses It. It merely means that we have no exclusive use of the Law of Life. It is important that you should be well, happy and successful, but these are effects, flowing from the mountain top of your vision where you have learned to speak the real creative word—the word of real power, the word of Life, because it is a word of unity.

In actual practice here is an example of what this means:

> Someone comes to you and says, "I would like you to use your word to demonstrate friendship for me."
>
> What is going to be your pattern of thought? Surely not this man's loneliness or unhappiness. Your pattern of thought must exclude these undesirable qualities and include the rhythm of life, the unity of every person in the One, the One flowing through all.

*You start with the realization* that there is but One Life Principle. All people exist in this One, therefore everyone is already spiritually unified with everyone else.

*Here you enter into the use* of the word of great power. You have climbed the mountain of realization, of unity, and in this ascent you have dropped from your shoulders the burden of your friend's anxiety, the weight of his sense of loneliness. You have let go of his sense of separation and isolation. You have climbed steadily until you view the spiritual world of which he is a definite part.

*Now you are going to declare,* to decree, to affirm, that he is one with everyone.

Having done this you may rest in quiet confidence that, because of the statements you have made, this man will now find love and friendship everywhere he turns. Make this a positive affirmation and accept it completely. Your word, now acting as law, will automatically bring about the demonstration. It will be a demonstration for him and not for someone else because you have consciously directed the Law for his particular need. Every sense of personal responsibility should be eliminated and you should rest in a quiet contemplation of the meaning of the words you have spoken. The Law will bring about the desired result.

Again, someone may ask you to go up into your

mountain for the realization of abundance. Perhaps you may have to clear your thought of the belief that he must remain in poverty, ill luck, lost opportunity, etc. Always speak your words of affirmation and denial with clear, positive conviction. Passing through this stage of thought, having let the burden of his sense of impoverishment fall from your shoulders, you have reached a place in your mind where you realize that Substance is everywhere, because the Life Principle is everywhere.

When you have reached this conclusion, calmly state:

> *This man is directed by Divine Intelligence.*
> *He is governed by Infinite Wisdom.*
> *He is propelled into right action.*
> *His thought and imagination are saturated*
>     *by an Intelligence which at all times*
>     *knows what he ought to do, which at all*
>     *times guides him.*

Your responsibility is to proclaim the truth for him, and with Browning exclaim, "With God be the rest!"

Suppose someone says to you, "Please help me to gain better health." Again you are to make the ascent into your mountain where the word of Life exists. Possibly, you may meet certain obstructions of thought which call for certain affirmations and denials. These affirmations and denials clear your pathway in the ascent, for you are to arrive at a realization that the essence of this man—the life, truth and reality about him—is pure Being.

You are to reach a place where you think of him as part of the Whole, perfect in the Whole, one with It. As a result of your word a new flow of life will start from the Center of his being. You are not creating this Center nor starting the flow, you are merely recognizing his true being, declaring it to be there, with full confidence that it will manifest in his experience.

If you cling to processes as simple as these, you cannot fail. You are assuming no personal responsibility, you are transferring the whole burden into the Law. You are recognizing that there is a divine, creative pattern in Life, a perfect spiritual prototype of this man's being. His thought has been flowing from the belief that he is isolated, separated, apart from his good, whether it be health, happiness or success. He has been speaking a limited word, and unless your consciousness reaches a level higher than the one from which he has been thinking, you will do him no good.

In working for yourself or others, if you can transcend the thoughts which deny the true individuality and arrive at a realization of the meaning of the true self, you can always speak a word more powerful than that which has produced any negative condition or situation.

We are surrounded by an impersonal Law which operates upon our personal word. This is the whole secret. This is why we are taught that the Law flows from the word. This is true whether we think of it as the creation of the whole universe by the Word of Life, or whether we think of those lesser creations which we would like to project upon the screen of our moving experience.

We all desire to enter into a greater degree of livingness. There is nothing wrong about this. It is only because we have a limited idea that the Law limits us. The creative soil does not know that a squash is larger than a peanut. So the Law of the Power, with which we are dealing, automatically operates upon our ideas whether we think of them as big or little. We want to so combine our use of the Law, which is impersonal, with our personal word, directing the Law, that the greatest possible good shall follow.

If we do this we shall no longer cry, "Why hast thou forsaken me?" for we shall have discovered that God has never been absent from our lives for one single moment. The Divine has never withdrawn Itself from our presence; Love has never deserted us. We shall discover that we are and always have been immersed in this Thing called Life, closer than breathing, nearer than hands and feet, as intimate as our own thoughts, as personal to us as our own breath. We shall discover that our freedom is built upon a foundation so broad that even the passing limitations of our experience, and the anguish of our minds, were included in this freedom.

We shall be like the prodigal son who, returning to his father's house, was amazed that the father came forth to meet him; that Divine Protection placed on his shoulders the seamless robe of perfection, while Divine Bounty welcomed him with a table spread with the gifts of Life. The father had never deserted him at all; he had merely wandered into a far land; he had imagined himself separated from his good.

We shall also be like the prodigal's brother who complained that he had remained in the father's house laboring, but that the father had not spread a table for him that he might entertain his friends. For the Father will also say to us, "Son, thou art ever with me, and all that I have is thine."

The cry, "Why hast thou forsaken me?" will be lost in the exalted concept that "they that dwell in the secret place of the most High shall abide under the shadow of the Almighty."

We must seek the Source of Life if we would live, and no longer seeing as through a glass darkly, we shall be gently led from our canyons of disillusionment into the fertile valleys of peace through which flows the River of Life. Being individuals, the choice is ours. Being divine, we seek freedom; being immortal, we shall find it.